GRACE GOLDIN

WORK OF MERCY

A PICTURE HISTORY OF HOSPITALS

ASSOCIATED
MEDICAL SERVICES

THE BOSTON MILLS
PRESS

CANADIAN CATALOGUING IN PUBLICATION DATA

Goldin, Grace
Work of Mercy: a pictorial history of hospitals

ISBN 1-55046-118-4

1. Hospitals – History.
2. Hospitals – History – Pictorial works.
3. Hospital care – History.
4. Hospital care – History – Pictorial works.
I. Title

RA964-G65 1994   362.1'1'09   C94-930629-0

Sponsored by:
Associated Medical Services, Inc.
14 Prince Arthur Avenue, Toronto
Ontario, Canada M5R 1A9
Tel: 416 924 3368
Fax: 416 323 3338

Published by:
The Boston Mills Press
132 Main Street, Erin
Ontario, Canada N0B 1T0
Tel: 519 833 2407
Fax: 519 833 2195

Distributed by:
Stoddart Publishing Company Limited
34 Lesmill Road, Toronto
Ontario, Canada M3B 2T6
Tel: 416 445 3333
Fax: 416 445 5967

Design by:
Ivan Holmes Design, Toronto

Printed and bound in Hong Kong

Frontispiece
Archives, Ospedale degli' Innocenti, Florence, Italy

Associated Medical Services, Incorporated is a charitable organization which, through its Board and the Hannah Institute for the History of Medicine, supports a wide range of scholarly activities related to the history of medicine and medical education in Canada.

For three friends who cared most that this book be published

Ruth Eisenstein

Thérèse Romer

Sheila Snelgrove

CONTENTS

FOREWORD

In this fascinating collection of inspired photographs and inspired text, which carries her considerable scholarship very lightly, Grace Goldin takes us through a largely unexplored area of social history. Centres of care, hospices and hospitals, were built by the Church throughout Western Europe during the Middle Ages, welcoming generations of the sick poor, forming what almost amounted to a National Health Service. She has brought to life not only their beautiful architecture and homely details but also those who suffered, died and worked in them. Single figures and worn faces stand in for their countless patients, carers and humble helpers. They light up the accompanying collections of plans and drawings and help us to enter some of the heritage from which our modern medical care has developed. It also shows compellingly the humanity which can be sadly swamped by the enormous developments and discoveries of today's hospitals.

In looking at the modern hospice Grace Goldin has matched wards and buildings with a higher proportion of portraits, those of patients and and those working with them. By doing this she has emphasized that today's hospice teams (often working with the patient and family in their own homes) are accepting death more honestly than many a hospital nurse or doctor and are thus able to relate closely to people as they face this important time of life. The public may now add "for the dying" to the word hospice, but those within its care are helped to be concerned with living as fully as they can until they die, according to their own important values. Liveliness as well as peace is caught here in both group and individual pictures.

Since her journey around a number of English hospices with their varied approaches, much thought has come together to develop further the hospice concept both in the U.K. and around the world. It can be summed up, "Here we are concerned with the whole man – body, mind and spirit – part of some family unit, with physical and practical needs for us to tackle with maximum competence." That competence has developed fast since St. Christopher's opened its wards in 1967 and set out in Home Care in 1969. Other centres have joined in developing a widely recognized body of research into the relief of physical and family distress. There has been a broader look at spiritual need than that comprised entirely by religious belief and practice, and its workers believe that as they themselves search for meaning in often desperate situations, they can help to create a climate in which patients and families make their own individual discoveries. No longer does hospice set out to help people think exactly as their often Christian foundations suggest, rather the aim is that they should think as deeply as they can in their own way.

St. Christopher's Hospice has found that this wider look at the whole spiritual dimension has been built up from the creativity and growth of many of its patients and witnesses to the discovery of their own strengths by countless families. It has also developed through the experience of its staff, a community of the unlike. The same is true of many other centres and is illustrated in this book by some fascinatingly diverse comments from hospice workers.

Many of the older Europeans hospices have become almshouse for the elderly, as we see in some of the photographs. In consequence, the Palliative Care Unit or Team is here a more common title, as it is in some other parts of the world. We may regret the apparent loss of the full meaning of "hospice," the giving of total hospitality, but so long as the true human dimension is recognized and met on a personal level, perhaps we can say "What's in a name?" and be glad that something of the spirit so beautifully saluted here has grown up to redress the balance of today's emphasis on technology. Hospice influence has spread far beyond its own origins and this book deserves to do the same.

Dame Cicely Saunders OM., DBE., FRCP.

PREFACE

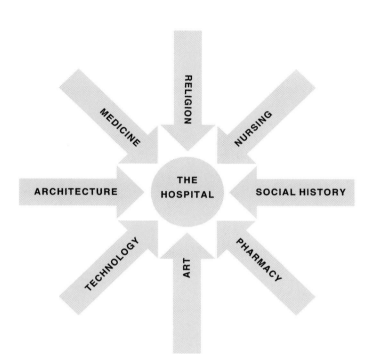

Hospitals are places where a lot of people from different backgrounds gather and mingle. The common denominator among these people is illness – some suffer from it, some try to make it go away. Hospitals are also the meeting-place of many disciplines. This diagram shows the principal ones: medicine, nursing, pharmacy, architecture, technology, religion, art, social history. If you think about the history of hospitals – which most of us don't – you realize that the hospital is where ideas from many different fields must meet and mingle.

This book, in words and pictures, is a selection of the richest materials collected during twenty years of visits to old hospitals, and a digging among primary and secondary sources to learn about them. It reflects a search for a telling detail in the pictures, a delightful story from the texts.

The history, broadly speaking, traces religious – i.e. Catholic – motivations behind medieval hospitals in Europe (it does not go to Asia, Africa, South America); it reflects the importance in all ages of good nursing care; the tardiness of a medical impact on hospital techniques – or on home cures, for that matter, for there was no effective medicine until the 19th century, when there was a growing preoccupation, from mid-century on, with a sanitary environment (at last!).

The skin of the hospital, the architectural style in which it was dressed, changed from century to century and from country to country as fashions in clothes do; very few were the fundamental concerns that shaped the structure of the buildings. Efficiency was a factor in the Middle Ages, but had more to do with making sure that a patient could see the performance of the Mass, than with merely saving money. Then there was (and is) the question of single rooms. For reasons not hard to comprehend, in every century these rooms went to the rich, to the contagious, or to the mad. In the last half of the 19th century thoroughgoing architectural reforms powerfully reflect the desire for a sanitary environment, and in the present century saving money shapes the hospital as much as the determination to save lives – now that it is medically possible to do so.

In the recent preoccupation with medical procedures of real helpfulness but extraordinary complexity, direct contact with patients as human beings was often lost, a loss modern hospices for the dying were created to correct. Hospices in that sense are a return to medieval care (as opposed to cure) institutions.

Now how did I, to whom every hospital field was foreign territory, find myself involved in such a history? With not one relevant discipline was I familiar, in not one was I trained. They rose as obstacles to block my path to reasonable comprehension of these vast, intricate, fascinating multi-disciplinary institutions, and each had to be at least sketchily understood.

In 1963, I was invited by John D. Thompson of Yale to find out what happened in nursing ward design before Florence Nightingale went to the Crimea. He was preparing efficiency studies dealing with the mid-20th century nursing ward, or inpatient unit as it is called. I began to learn what a hospital is and does, both new and old. Twelve years later, in 1975, *The Hospital, A Social and Architectural History*, by Thompson and Goldin, was published by the Yale University Press. The book's first 250 pages are my history of the evolution of the nursing ward. The last 75 pages are his nursing efficiency studies. That book is now out of print, and I reproduce in this one a few of its illustrations and some sections of my text.

As preparation I went each summer to visit European hospitals, the earliest from 1142, the latest some unfinished British hospices for the dying. Most of the time I followed itineraries generously worked out for me by the dean of modern hospital historians, Dieter Jetter of Köln. Usually traveling alone, I drew the line at the Iron Curtain, but visited at least one hospital, generally many more, in every country of Western Europe except Finland and Portugal – omissions I regret.

Innumerable hospital administrators opened their doors and let me photograph literally from cellar to rooftop, but they would often not permit portraits of patients. I had to imagine occupants in beds from the layout of wards however decrepit or reconstructed they might be. I did however find two visual aids. Pictures of past centuries represent hospital interiors of their time with startling vividness and more or less reasonable fidelity. And at St. Christopher's Hospice, London, which I first visited three years after it opened in 1963, and at least a dozen times since (as well as – once each – some 26 other modern British hospices for the dying), I found a patient population similar to that of the Middle Ages, people who could only be cared for, not cured, and to whom one might offer the consolations of religion. But hospice patients of today are luckier than those in the old hospice. Now we are better able to control pain.

In medical museums of each country were old prints, plans and documents to photocopy. I have at least 10,000 color slides and 15,000 black-and-white and color negatives relating to the history of hospitals, both my own views and the copy work. This book contains the best and most interesting.

Along the way I acquired superb teachers, counselors, sponsors, friends, whom I shall list leaving off degrees, titles, descriptions, and even whether these people are living or dead – I cannot do justice in this space to their contributions to their fields nor to their very diverse and invaluable contributions to this book. They are: Hans Burkens, William F. Bynum, William A. Christian, Jr., Kenneth J. Conant, Judah Goldin, Ferenc Gyorgyey, Miles Hardie, Robert Herrlinger, Jane Isay, Robert J.T. Joy, George Kubler, Erna Lesky, Peter Neubauer, George Rosen, Cicely Saunders, Richard Shryock, Egill Snorrason, Lloyd Stevenson, Ian Sutton, Charles H. Talbot, Edward Tenner, Elizabeth Thomson, and Juliette Vanderschueren. Names, sometimes portraits, of other helpers appear in the text – and there are so many others who remain nameless! Special thanks to Douglas Waugh, editor, and to Leonard Wilson for reviewing this book in manuscript. With all the good help given, I claim the remaining mistakes as my own.

This book would never have been published were it not for the sponsorship of Associated Medical Services Incorporated of Canada and its President, Donald R. Wilson, as well as the Hannah Institute for the History of Medicine. It further owes a tremendous debt to the coordination of Sheila Snelgrove, and to the extraordinary gifts of its designer, Ivan Holmes. To all involved, my profound thanks.

After *The Hospital* was published I organized unused sections of my collection as scholarly papers, for publication in the Journal of the History of Medicine and Allied Sciences, the Bulletin of the History of Medicine, and the Encyclopedia Britannica Medical and Health Annual. These essays have never appeared in book form and are extensively reproduced in the present text.

My first photographic exhibit was at the Harvey Cushing Rotunda, Yale Medical Library, in 1969. It later went to the Woodward Biomedical Library, University of British Columbia, in Vancouver. Many slide lectures followed in the United States, Canada, and Europe. Then a greatly expanded exhibit of 18 panels, 346 photographs (mostly in color) was mounted in 1983, under the sponsorship of Leonard Wilson, at the Owen H. Wangensteen Historical Library of Biology and Medicine, University of Minnesota, Minneapolis. It traveled to the National Library of Medicine (sponsor, James Cassedy) and National Institute of Pathology, Washington D.C., the Biomedical Library, Center for the Health Sciences, UCLA (sponsor, Dora Weiner), and the University of Iowa Hospitals, Iowa City, before being bought for the permanent collection at the University of Chicago Hospitals in 1986, where it can be seen today.

So successful was this exhibit that a second version of it was sent to Canada in 1986, where it travelled from coast to coast and back during five years under the joint sponsorship of the Associated Medical Services of Canada, Inc. and the Hannah Institute for the History of Medicine. A third version opened in 1988 at the Annual Meetings of the American Association for the History of Medicine in New Orleans and, having traveled here and there in the United States for four years, was bought for the permanent collection at Stanford University Hospital, Berkeley, California.

This book is chiefly based on that later exhibit. It is the distillation of nearly a quarter century's immersion in the history of hospitals. From it a compelling conclusion inevitably arises: we cannot afford to be complacent. The old hospitals were the best our forefathers could do. In the absence of real medical insights, they had to cope somehow with helpless sufferers. Where we know a cure that they did not, their efforts seem primitive and irrational, of mere historic interest. But when no cure is known, or a new disease surfaces – AIDS replacing plague or tuberculosis, for example – we are likely to react as they did, with panic, bewilderment, and tangled impulses.

Historic hospitals may be an acquired taste, but there is much to recommend them. As a destination for travel: the town might be a tourist trap, but you will be welcome in the old hospital (always excepting Beaune, where the old hospital is the tourist trap). As a field of research: compared to English literature, say, whose every line is claimed and quarrelled over by three or four specialists, hospital history is an almost empty field – the middle of the Arizona desert as compared to the island of Manhattan. As a project for conservation: to record, to preserve (even some of the hospitals recorded here are no longer with us), and to admire, for many are beautiful. What shows in this book is but a drop in the bucket. So many historic hospitals are out there waiting: others in the countries of Western Europe that are represented here, and all those beyond the Iron Curtain; in India, the Far East, and especially in the Arab world. Old ones in Canada; emphatically those in South and Central America. Wherever they are, they're mouldering fast, and they are irreplaceable. Someone starting out, with good feet and the strength to lug tripod, copier, lenses and cameras, should carry on where this book leaves off.

The book does aim to persuade future photographers and hospital historians to take up an exciting challenge. But in the larger sense it is meant much more for stay-at-homes doing their work in one of the disciplines: doctors, nurses, architects; historians of these three fields and of art; social historians; certainly those interested in religion and history of religion, particularly Catholicism. Finally, the book is meant for every patient who ever lay in hospital wondering not only, "How did I get here?" but, "How did it get here?"

INTRODUCTION

They are so old, these hospitals, so old... What does a really old hospital look like? Quite simply, like other architecture of its time and place. For instance, the refectory of the Hospital of the Knights of St. John, Acco (Acre), Israel, dating from the 13th century, is a Romanesque hall recently "excavated" by removing rubble that over the centuries had filled it to within six feet of the ceiling.

The rear wall (on the river side) of the Hospital del Marcos, Gandía, Spain, gives evidence of periodic remodeling over the centuries. This is typical of old hospitals. I know nothing more about this hospital except that, in 1960, all its wastes were thrown into the nearby river, without hesitation.

2   Rear wall, Hospital del Marcos, Gandía, Spain   1   Refectory, Hospital of St. John, Acco, Israel, 13th century

The Ospedale di Sant'Antonio, Lastra-Signa near Florence, Italy, still stands just inside the city gate, in a typical location of a hostel-hospital, intended as much for wayfarers as for the sick. The Lastra-Signa city wall dates back to 1380, the hospice was founded in 1411. By 1970, the ground-floor chapel of the hospice had been abandoned, but in the rooms above someone still lived, as witness the bird-cage and striped curtain. The arches of the arcade predate Brunelleschi's "pioneering" ones at the Ospedale degli'Innocenti of Florence by eight years.

This is the river façade of one of many Santo Spirito hospitals, the Hôpital de St. Esprit, the river being made use of in both its aspects: upstream as a water source, and downstream as a sewer.

3   Ospedale di Sant'Antonio, Lastra-Signa, Italy, 1411

4   Hôpital de St. Esprit, Besançon, France, 15th century

Now, what is to be done with or about the historic, mean-
ingful, outgrown, crumbling architectural shell of an old
hospital, with this important evidence of bygone care-tak-
ers, patients, and methods of cure long obsolete?

Many fates befall an old hospital.

The Heilig-Geist-Spital (another version of the Holy
Ghost) of Nürnberg, Germany (1339), which expanded over
the Peignitz river as a bridge when no other direction for
expansion was available, was totally demolished during
World War II and rebuilt according to the original plan —
but made homogeneous. The texture of individual, step-by-
step, century-by-century construction was quite lost.

5   Heilig-Geist-Spital, Nürnberg, Germany, 1339, before World War II

6   Heilig-Geist-Spital, Nürnberg, Germany, as rebuilt after World War II

Preservationists try to save an old building by diverting it to new and different use. In their very old age there were changes in function in many: the Hospital de Santa Cruz, Toledo, Spain (1514) was converted to an art museum; the open wards of the Hospital de la Santa Creu, Barcelona (15th-17th century) became a library and cultural center; the Pest House of Leiden, Netherlands (1661) is now a military museum. And so it goes.

The Hospital of Montblanch, a small town near Tarragona, Spain, was turned into an apartment house which is the part of it we see here. The church next door – out of sight to the right – had been allowed to fall into decay.

7   Courtyard, Hospital, Montblanch, Spain, 16th century

Some hospitals still function with surprisingly little change. This nurse at the Hospital de la Caridad, Seville, Spain (founded 1664) was dipping water from the well in 1969 for use in the wards behind her. An unaltered state might suggest that there were no funds to renovate and that a need persisted. In this case, however, excellent oil paintings by Murillo executed especially for this hospital can now be seen in the hospital church – for a fee. Thus is maintained the present old men's home.

The nun dipping water can represent all the nuns who ever nursed at the Caridad. But older than the Hospital del Rey of Burgos, Spain, founded in the 12th century, is the eternal figure of this washerwoman, who represents all the humble folk who ever did the wash, mopped the floors, emptied the chamber pots and stoked the stoves in hospitals all over the world.

8   Courtyard, Hospital de la Caridad, Seville, Spain, 1664

9   Washerwoman, Hospital del Rey, Burgos

PART ONE

HOSPITALS AND CHRISTIANITY

A soldier exclaimed in admiration : "I would not do that work for one hundred francs an hour."—"And I," said the Brother Infirmarian,—"I would not do it for a million ; but for God's sake I do it with pleasure."

10   The *Ambulance* (field hospital) of St.Claude-les-Besançon, France

1 THE CHRISTIAN HOSPITAL

How did an old hospital ward look when in full activity? Much like the one in this print by Philippe Thomassin. Hospitals at the end of the 16th century – and even until the middle of the 19th century – were not the least like those we know today. They were not sanitary machines – indeed, they were not sanitary. Nor were they medically oriented, since physicians could not cure. There were no short-term patients: if patients didn't die in hospital, they were likely to catch a secondary disease which detained them. Economy meant something different in those days since most patients were charity cases. The real payment for devoted medical and nursing services was a heavenly reward.

The hospital Thomassin chose to portray is probably not any particular one, but all the more useful to us for being generic. About the only similarity to the hospitals we know is that there are patients in beds. Men and women are separated – men on the right, women on the left. They lie naked, save for the turbans or bed-caps on the women. Food is being served at the lower left, and drink as well midway down on the right. Further to the rear what is proffered may be medication. In the second bed on the left, medical treatment is in progress – a woman is being bled, from a vein on the inner arm near the elbow. In this idyllic scene, patients lie singly in beds wide enough for two. More often they lay two to a bed in beds we would think only fit for one.

The dominant feature of this scene is an altar, and a patient is praying at it. From such scant evidence of medical treatment, what other hope was there? Behind the altar is a painting of the Good Samaritan. To ensure that you don't overlook it, a man is pointing to the Samaritan. For this, like all hospitals of the time, was a charity hospital, and the patients in the beds are paupers. Rich folk were nursed at home by their families. The poor were nursed by Christian charity and fed by Christian alms.

St. Chrysostom said, "If there were no poor, the greater part of your sins would not be remedied; they are the healers of your wounds."

On these points a second interior scene is even more explicit. It shows (below) the 16th century Spanish saint, Juan de Dios, John of God, now the patron saint of hospitals, washing the feet of the Christ. The legendary story that accompanies it is that John has just brought a pauper, the latest of many, into his small hospital – note the two rows of beds with patients against the long walls, and the dim altar in the rear. John was the hospital ambulance, he lifted the poor beggar on his shoulders and carried him in. As usual, he washes the patient's feet before putting him to bed. He recognizes the stigmata. The house fills with a great light, waking the other patients who think the place is on fire. And John tells them to go back to sleep, it's all right.

"What you have done for the least of mine you have done for me," says his visitor. And John replies, "I have reflected upon your works and have become full of fear."

Above this scene, Pope Pius V issues a papal bull to John's successors, with the admonition, "Don't forget hospitality," or, "the hospital." In the clouds still higher up reside Faith with her cross, Hope with her anchor, Charity with her children, "and the greatest of them is Charity."

11 "The Fourth Work of Mercy is to Visit the Sick". Print by Philippe Thomassin, end of 16th century

How eloquently this room in the 17th century Infirmary of Byloke Hospital at Ghent in Belgium speaks of a prized duty! Patients came to the hospital hungry, dirty and footsore, if in no worse shape, and had the right to a square meal and a night's shelter at the very least. Before they were discharged, their feet were washed. It was a humble task, performed for the humblest – an exercise in humility much prized by the devout. This is the room where the feet of the poor were washed on Maundy Thursday, the day before

12   John of God washes the feet of the Christ

13   Room where the feet of the poor were washed on Maundy Thursday.
       Byloke Hospital, Ghent, Belgium, 17th century

I WAS HUNGRIE AND YEE
GAVE MEE MEATE. I WAS
THIRSTIE AND YEE GAVE MEE
DRINKE. I WAS NAKED AND
YEE CLOTHED MEE. I
WAS HARBARLES AND YEE
CAVE MEE LODGINGE. CUM
YEE BLESED OF MY FATHER
INHERIT THE KINGDUM
PREPARED FOR YOU.
MAT 25,
ANNO CHRI 1612 ET
ANNO REG IAC REGIS
MAGN BRITTAN IO.

The Seven Works of Mercy were the following:

To feed the hungry
To give drink to the thirsty
To clothe the naked
To visit the sick
To take in the stranger
To free the prisoners
To bury the dead

All but the last work are based on a New Testament text (Matthew 25:40). The last (from the *Book of Tobit*) was added in the 13th century. All but the next to last directly apply to the work of the medieval hospital, and together account for its extraordinary patient mix.

Good Friday. On that day the act was elevated to a prescribed ritual, and those performing it were the religious and secular leaders of the community. In the background is a painting by Schilduyen (1691) of Visiting the Sick – the Act of Mercy that has given us so many pictures of hospital interiors in bygone centuries.

14   The Seven Works of Mercy: an early English text

16   Vagabond warming himself by the fire, in a room behind the open ward of the Gasthuis of Gheel, Belgium, 1639

In early pictures of hospital interiors, it is hard to tell where allegory leaves off and a realistic portrayal begins, but a drawing by the Dutch artist, Johannes van Straaten, shows better than most what miscellany might result in a small hospital where – as in most small hospitals – the Seven Works of Mercy were taken as a guide.

From right to left: a head treatment; foreground center, possibly a patient being admitted, and to the left of him a patient dressing himself for discharge, behind him a woman is rising from her bed and a nurse runs with the communal cloak to cover her nakedness. Even the child is not out of place in a charity hospital, for the Works of Mercy led to hurly-burly admission of the homeless and starving, the acutely and chronically ill, the crippled, the aged, the blind, the mad, and helpless orphans. All humanity was admitted, in fact, save those recognized as contagious – lepers and the plague-ridden – who were isolated in separate institutions. Even a passing vagabond was entitled to one night's food and lodging.

15   Hospital Ward, Johannes van Straaten, 16th century

Over the door to the pharmacy of the Hôpital St. Jacques, Besançon, France, God the Father welcomes His Poor. Above the main gateway to the hospital is a cross, the date, 1709, and this message (Psalm 9:14 In the Douay, Ps. 10:14 in the Hebrew and King James versions of the Bible):

"To thee is the poor man left: thou wilt be a helper to the orphan."

Our Glorious Founders: their arms as they appear in the courtyard of the Caridad Hospital, Seville. It is generally assumed that a Founder contributed more than a Donor, or at least got there first with the gift. In 1791, John Howard reported from the Great Hospital of Genoa, Italy subtle differentiations in the hospital's acknowledgment of generosity:

The benefactors to this hospital are distinguished by the different postures and attitudes in which their statues are placed in the wards and on the staircase, according to the different sums which they have contributed. Many are placed standing, but an hundred thousand crowns entitles to a chair. I observed a statue which had one of the feet under the chair; and was told that the reason was that the benefactor honoured by it had contributed only ninety thousand crowns.

Lazarettos. 57

17   God the Father welcoming in His Poor. Pharmacy, Hôpital
     St. Jacques, Besançon, France

18   Founders' arms, Hospital de la Caridad, Seville, Spain

Some hospitals are rich, and possess treasures. Imagine what it means to the sisters of the Elizabeth Spital of Vienna (1836) to possess the purported skull of St. Elizabeth of Hungary (1207-31), the saint after whom the hospital is named! It is on the third storey of the hospital-church, safely locked in the sisters' cloister in an altar of its own, on which they may focus their devotion. Crowned, it rests on its own thigh bones, on crimson velvet with a little silver sliver where the tongue would be, and it wears a crown.

One last exhibit: an original fourteenth century hospital bed, from the Ospedale del Ceppo, Pistoia, Italy – now to be found in a niche of the neighboring Church of Santa Maria della Grazie. This is the story attached to it:

For fourteen years a young girl of Pistoia languished on this bed, and the only medicine which did her any good was the prayer to the Virgin, Salus Infirmorum. One day the Virgin did descend, and stopped by the bed of the young invalid, who immediately regained her vigor and a good

color. The Virgin, desiring an authoritative witness, sent some boys attracted by her splendor to call the priest. But the priest was hearing confessions and paid no attention to them. The Virgin insisted, adding that the Father had better preach the ordering of souls, for plague was coming to Pistoia and within a month he too would die. This brought the priest on the run. He arrived just in time to see her disappear.

"But her image remained on the wall over the bed, from which the sick child arose, fresh as a rose, and pure as a lily."

So they saved the bed. And the original bedclothes, too.
There was, from the bottom up:
A layer of boards
A mattress of wool
A mattress of straw
Another mattress of wool
Two bolsters, and the red bedspread.

20   14th century bed, Ospedale del Ceppo, Pistoia, Italy

2 THE WARD-CHAPEL COMBINATION

The connection between the ward of an historic Christian hospital and its chapel is best explained by three pictures executed in *azulejos*, colored tiles, at the original Hospital de la Santa Creu, Barcelona. Now used as a library, it consists of three huge halls running into one another in a C-formation; these were the wards. Off one of them are two small rooms, dated 1635, that I construe as having been meant for the dying. The first is appropriately decorated with the Stations of the Cross: "He suffered as I do now; maybe more." At the four corners of a second room are larger scenes, one, appropriately, a Last Judgement. The three others specifically address the patients of this or any hospital of the time.

Here is a dying woman whose destination is clear. A huge good angel triumphantly displays a scroll of her good deeds, while a tiny devil with a shorter list, despairing, leaps back into hell fire. Above the door we see her reception in heaven. She is to be dressed for glory. Her eyes are fixed on that vision and her face is confident.

Here is her opposite number. This man is going straight to hell. Four separate devils are at work on him. One points the spear, and he is reinforced by a Christ sitting in judgement. One manacles his ankles, while a sort of serpent immobilizes his arm. One reads out his evil deeds from the book of his life, and the fourth, carrying a torch, conducts his body toward the fiery door of hell. The nursing brother, who tried in vain to convert him, and his good angel sadly leave the scene. Death, the skeleton, triumphs.

The third picture depicts a real struggle. The devil is full-sized, but solitary, and he is being driven off by a militant angel with "I.H.S." on his shield. The nursing brother is

21 A Virgin and Child, even on the handle of the front door. Potterie Hospital, Bruges, Belgium, 1530

22 Death of a Good Woman, Hospital de la Santa Creu, Barcelona, 1635

23 Death of a Wicked Man, Hospital de la Santa Creu, Barcelona, 1635

that there was no doctoring we would think worthy of the name. None came to the hospital till they had to. Very often they came to die. The hospital had to provide for a good death – what hope was there but in the Life to Come? A good Christian had to die shriven. Thus it was essential that patients see, or at least hear, the Mass. In the early 13th century, 1210 to be specific, the elevation of the Host was delayed until after the priest took the bread for consecration. This assumed such importance in the mind of the faithful that, says Amiot, "those who had not seen the elevation imagined that they had not heard Mass. Sometimes people came to church merely for that..." If this was so for the general congregation, how much more passionately important the sight of the elevation must have been to patients who knew themselves about to die!

on his knees, and behind him is Christ, bearing a fleur-de-lis. Death, decently robed and seemingly crowned with a garland, smiles as encouraging and sociable a smile as was ever seen on a skeleton. Heaven awaits. This must have been a deathbed conversion, a triumph for the hospital. Cure the body if you can and care for it if you must – but above all, save souls!

We know that our hospital patient was very poor, and

Here is doctrine translated into architecture. This is the barrel-roofed Hôpital des Fontenilles of Tonnerre, France, 1293, one of the oldest hospitals to be seen in this book.

The ward is dark, compared to the chapel.

The ward ceiling is of wood, the chapel ceiling of stone, and of a sacred form.

The window of the chapel is also larger and of a sacred form, compared to the windows of the ward. The German hospital historian, Dieter Jetter, reminds us that while the

24   Deathbed Conversion, Hospital de la Santa Creu, Barcelona, 1635   25   Ward interior, Hôpital des Fontenilles, Tonnerre, France, 1293

ward window glass would have been colorless, as it is today, the altar glass was originally stained, thus the quantity of light – though not its quality – would have been more evenly distributed.

The original glass of the altar was recently fished up out of an old well and pieced together, thus we have a more or less contemporary portrait of the founder of this hospital, the widow-queen Marguerite de Bourgogne, sister-in-law of Louis IX.

The hospital was founded to atone for her sins during her married life and, as she put it, "with a desire to merit that reward the Evangelist has promised us." Her own dwelling stood beside the hospital, connected to it by a little bridge at second-storey (that is, balcony) level. A walkway at the base of the huge ward windows permitted her to look down on the patients in their beds. From remnants of wood in the side walls we know that each bed was in an alcove, perhaps resembling those in the reconstruction drawn by the 19th century French architect, Viollet-le-Duc. From the walkway one could adjust the ward windows (otherwise completely out of reach, and the steps leading up to them meaningless).

27   Chapel and ward windows, Tonnerre

26   (Left to right) Chapel and ward vaulting. Hôpital des Fontenilles
       Tonnerre, France, 1293

28   Marguerite de Bourgogne, Hôpital des Fontenilles, Tonnerre, France

29   Queen Marguerite de Bourgogne supervises patients. Tonnerre,
       France

On the outside of these windows two little holes are just visible, below the sills. They were a hygienic device: in this cold stone building, steam would naturally condense on the insides of the windows and run down them to the inner sills, whence the water was to be drained off by the two little holes in the stone.

Yet another hygienic device was the cloverleaf ventilation holes in the wooden slats of the ward ceiling, venting into the attic. The ward had a barrel-roofed ceiling and the attic had a peaked roof; the space between the two, the attic itself, was seen as a vast reservoir of fresh air.

This sundial is on the outer wall of the ward at the Hôpital des Fontenilles, Tonnerre.

31   Rear view of the peaked roof of the Hôpital des Fontenilles, Tonnerre; the chapel windows face us, the ward is behind them.

32   Ventilation holes in the ward ceiling, Hôpital des Fontenilles, Tonnerre

30   Drainage holes, Hôpital des Fontenilles, Tonnerre, France

33   Sundial, Hôpital des Fontenilles, Tonnerre, France

The Hôtel-Dieu of Beaune (also known as the Hospice de Beaune) is the best-known old hospital in the world. It has become a tourist site, vying with the wines of Beaune as a source of income for the town. Essentially a ward-chapel combination like the one at Tonnerre 150 years earlier, it has been extensively restored. No one knows how beds originally stood or what they looked like. I have chosen Tonnerre, as more pristine and less well-known than Beaune, to represent the type.

A ward-chapel combination is recognizable on sight from the exterior. This is St. Petronilla's at Bury St. Edmunds, England, 14th century, described by Rotha Mary Clay as "a cottage hospital for (female) lepers – the chapel and hall were under one roof."

34   Looking from ward to chapel, Hôtel-Dieu, Beaune, France, 1443

35   St. Petronilla's Hospital, Bury St. Edmunds, England, 14th century

St. Catharinagasthuis, Gouda, Netherlands, reflected in its canal: chapel 1400, ward building 1665 (restored). This ward building, in two stories, has only two rooms across the canal façade, but from there some dozen rooms run rearward, large and small (for the sick and aged). A ward-chapel combination may be large or small, a single open hall or multiple rooms; neither the nationality nor the patient mix makes any difference.

36   St. Catharinagasthuis, Gouda, Netherlands

Sometimes the ward and its chapel might be found in two buildings. The Infirmary of the Church of the Holy Ghost in Copenhagen runs into the church, and is attached to it, just as monks' *dortoirs* (dormitories) were attached, yet separate, in monasteries. This complex is a restored version of a 15th century original.

The infirmary might be a free-standing building, as here at the Abbey of Ourscamp, France, 1210. In that case it would be placed behind and a little to the right of the apse of the Abbey Church. The "Salle des Morts," as it was called, was kept in good physical condition because it was regularly used as a parish church, even after the destruction of the Abbey. There is no indication of a chapel within the Salle des Morts. The Abbey Church was its Chapel – a ward-chapel combination writ large.

37   Church of the Holy Ghost, Copenhagen, Denmark, 15th-16th century

38   Abbey of Ourscamp, France, 1210

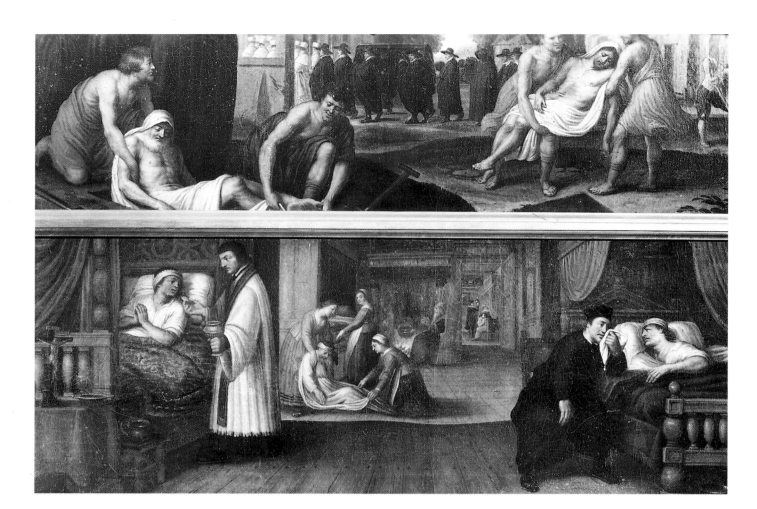

The function of three tiers of windows at Ourscamp is interesting. The rose window and the two large windows below it in the group do not open, and were used only for light. The small windows at person-level opened for ventilation. The sacred and secular functions of a hospital ward – saving souls, and curing bodies – could not be better expressed symbolically than by such a window arrangement.

The Maison de Coëffort in Le Mans is almost identical in form, outside and inside, to the Salle des Morts, yet the Salle des Morts was a monastic infirmary, while the Le Mans institution was both private and secular. The type of sponsorship does not determine the form of old hospital architecture.

A painting by van Oost from a church in Bruges defines the really important aspect of hospital care. On the right in the lower picture, a dying patient is being confessed, the confessor holds up a piece of cloth to cover all but his eyes and in that gesture transforms the bed to a confessional. The priest on the left comes with chalice and wafer: absolution.

In the upper picture is another Work of Mercy: Burying the Dead.

40   Deathbed confession, Burying the Dead. Paintings by van Oost in
      Bruges, 17th century

39   Interior, Salle des Morts, Ourscamp, France

3 THE HOSPICES CIVILS OF STRASBOURG

Some historic hospitals were built on a grand plan from the outset, though there was usually not quite enough money to complete so grand a design. Two examples of both the ambition and the falling short are the Ospedale Maggiore of Milan in the 15th century and Johns Hopkins Hospital of Baltimore in the 19th, both of which will be discussed later on. Normal hospital development, however, was more like that of a town which starts with one or two settler's families, one little house or a group of houses, and expands slowly.

The Hospices Civils of Strasbourg, Alsace, was such an institution, growing by well-documented degrees. We can set aside a legendary founding date of 657, though more sober fact presumes the existence of a hospital after 1100, when the first bishop took over. Bishops had been given the poor as their personal responsibility, so they built the first town hospitals. Written record begins in 1143 and tells us that the first and second bishops had ceded more land to the poor of the hospital on the Street of the Old Hospital, suggesting an existing building, a First Hospital, whose dates have been set at 1118-1316. Only its chapel appears on a town plan of 1548, more than 200 years after it had ceased to be used as a hospital chapel. On the plan its modest portal still opens upon the Street of the Old Hospital, and a tiny apse of four windows can be made out at its rear.

After 1143, the First Hospital no longer took in the sick, only poor pensioners. This first hospital was destroyed by a great fire in 1298, all but the building with the apse.

Since there was no room for expansion within the town walls, the Second Hospital was built outside them – four new buildings and a chapel, surrounded by a wall (n). A Chapel of the Precious Blood (m) was built in the midst of the cemetery. (Essential appendage, that cemetery.) This complex was located across the river from the town wall and gate (34); a location just within or outside the town wall was typical of hospitals. In 1319 the pensioners moved in.

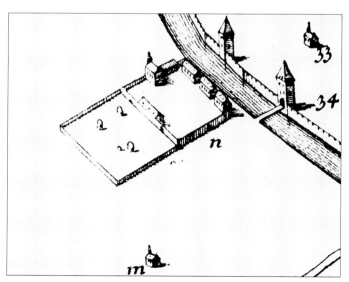

42   Chapel of the First Hospital (c. 1118) as it appears on a plan of 1548, Hospices Civils, Strasbourg

43   The Second Hospital, 1316, Hospices Civils, Strasbourg

41   Rooftops, Hospices Civils, 18th century, Strasbourg, France

The walled garden behind the hospital square gave them their groceries, and the orchard, represented by three trees, their fruit.

The second hospital was razed. Any buildings outside the town walls could hide from view an approaching enemy. It was relocated again within the walls, behind the "Porte de l'Hôpital" with its tower (from which the hospital roof was photographed). A drawing of 1576, from the south, of hospital and double town wall indicates gardens planted between the first wall and the second. We see, from left to right, the ward building, the chapel, and the tower of the hospital gate.

This third hospital, called the "New" or "Great" Hospital ("*magnum*", "*majus*") was completed in 1398. Of this building only the cellars remain. The rest perished in 1716, in another fire. A more realistic view of its ward building and chapel in 1673 does not neglect to record on the wall between ward and chapel a spidery construction that is not a sundial, but a reproduction and memorial of a mammoth human growth that had been excised by operation in this very hospital.

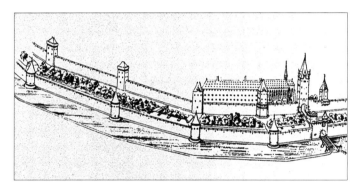

The hospital was rebuilt in the 18th century on the old plan. In 1795 its name was temporarily changed to "Hospital of the Bourgeois," "Hospice of Equality," just as the names of the months of the year were changed during the French Revolution. A center, square protuberance on its north facade today contains kitchens on every floor, the octagonal protuberance (behind a tree) a stack of toilets.

45   The Third Hospital in 1673, Hospices Civils, Strasbourg

44   The Third Hospital, 1576, Hospices Civils, Strasbourg

46

46   The Fourth Hospital in 1975

47   Interior of servant's room, Hospices Civils

48   Servants' corridor, Hospices Civils

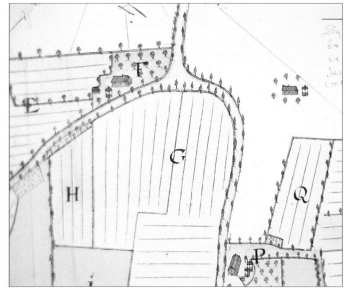

The roof windows were, of course, for the rooms for servants. The penniless and the help have always lived in garrets. Behind striped window shades of the lowest attic room to the right is nowadays a bed-sitter, approached from a long bare corridor: over the centuries, par for the course.

By contrast, the grand staircase; but this was a contrast to be seen in every wealthy home.

The original historic hospital still exists – underground. The *caves*, the cellars, are in this case true wine-cellars; ancient casks – the earliest dated 1472 – are still being used for mellowing wine, and the cellar, when I saw it in 1975, was a wine storage and bottling works.

What has a hospital to do with wine? Remember those dying patients? If they had no family to whom to bequeath their fortune and lands, if the hospital had taken them in in their last days, if they saw charity as a religious act; if, indeed, a legal arrangement had been worked out on admission between the old folk and the hospital, assuring them care for the rest of their days in return for all they owned – an arrangement not unknown even in nursing homes today – then it was but a step from taking care of the dying landowners to bottling the juice of their grapes.

The same thing happened at Beaune.

Here is one section of one plan (there was a whole book of them) representing real property belonging to St.Pieters-en-Bloklands Gasthuis, Amersfoort, Netherlands; every last house, tree, well and ploughed field accounted for.

The Bottle-end of the bottling works, Hospices Civils, Strasbourg. This cellar also has medical interest. The door-way, foreground right, leads to a windowless room that projects out under the street. In that room in the 18th century, even though it was illegal, dissections were performed.

50   One map of the holdings of St. Pieters-en-Bloklands Gasthuis, Amersfoort, Netherlands

51   Wine cellar, Hospices Civils, Strasbourg, France

49   Grand Staircase, Hospices Civils, Strasbourg

4 JOHN OF GOD AND HIS SPANISH HOSPITALS

"Once upon a time." This is how one is tempted to begin the life of Juan de Dios, John of God. So much fiction has mingled with the facts of his life that one cannot tell where truth leaves off and fantasy begins. We know he was born John Cuidad in Portugal in 1495, and died at Granada, Spain, 1550; was beatified in 1630 and canonized in 1690. It was only in 1886 that he was declared patron saint of hospitals and sick persons.

There is not much in the known facts to account for all those hospitals founded in his name! In 1572 Pope Pius V established the Order of John of God. A list drawn up in 1715, a little more than 150 years after the saint's death, credits to his Order 256 hospitals in Spain and Portugal, the New World, Italy and Sicily, France, Germany, and Poland, with 7,692 beds, serving 96,365 patients a year, in the care of 2,399 religious. In 1970 some of those totals had not changed much: 225 hospitals (for retarded and incurables,

as well as general care) with 2,300 brethren throughout the world. Now there are 50,000 beds. Whether the life of John of God as it has come down to us be fact or legend, or a mixture of both, his life was the first seed of all those hospitals.

Because John of God was a poor little man, his first hospital rose, so to speak, out of the naked earth. His charitable impulse broke through the hard soil like the impulse of a volcano choosing where to build its cone. John of God began his hospital-founding career by hauling filthy tramps into a single rented room and rummaging up firewood to thaw them out.

The art of building hospitals was by no means in its infancy in Spain when John stepped in with his makeshift arrangements. The Catholic Monarchs, Ferdinand and Isabella, erected during his lifetime a most elegant, minutely thought-out huge hospital for the sick and weary arriving in Santiago de Compostela, at the northwestern tip of Spain, a focus for pilgrimage from all over Europe. On so long a journey over poor roads, pilgrims arrived – if they ever did – at best in a state of collapse, at worst mortally ill. Royally commissioned, funded, and endowed, such a hospital could be built all in one place and at one time. The usual hospital, however, was likely to develop along the lines of the one John founded in Granada: first a single room, with himself as nurse; later, larger quarters and some staff would be added; finally and by degrees as money became available, a building of its own and an order of religious nurses. For the history of hospitals, the one John of God built at Granada is more representative and interesting than Compostela.

Spain was about to become a world power, thanks to gold from America. But this did not happen in John's life-

52 John of God weeps with compassion for all who suffer. From the altar of the church of the Hospital de S. Juan de Dios, Antequera, Spain

53 Court, looking toward dome of church, Hospital de S. Juan de Dios, Antequera, Spain, 1790

time. Nor would it have made much difference. Spain at the height of her power would not have attracted our saint, just because he was a saint. In the best of times he would have headed straight for the alleys and the forsaken ones. He was cut of the same cloth as St. Francis of Assisi, who kissed lepers, and St. Francis Xavier, who was said to have cleansed the ulcers of his patients with his tongue. St. Bernard of Clairvaux used to say that to go up and down the wards was like walking in fragrant gardens, and to deal with the sick was his greatest pleasure. In our time, we have Mother Theresa.

John had the asceticism of a saint. And not without measurable gains. "The blessed man would go about emaciated and yellow as the result of the life he led. This earned him respect and consideration as a man of God. Everyone called him John of God, and he would reply, 'If God wishes.'" He had the patience of a saint. An 18th century painting hanging in the arcade of a court of the Hospital of S. Juan de Dios in Granada illustrates his humility to perfection. The story goes that John collided with a nobleman in a narrow street and knocked off his cloak.

"Villainous scoundrel!" exclaimed the nobleman, "Why don't you watch where you're going?"

"Forgive me, brother, I wasn't looking where I was

going," John replied, making use of a moderately informal "you" form which, together with "brother," further incensed the nobleman and he slapped him.

"It is I who erred," said John of God, "for I well deserve it; give me another!"

Look well at the face of the saint. He has eyes in the back of his head; he sees the angel coming with the crown of roses. This is the man who signed his letters "the least brother of all the children of God." But this is also the man who used to say that there would be many of his habit in the ministry of the poor throughout the world.

John's first 46 years were unstable and adventurous. By turns shepherd and soldier, at one point in Africa he nearly converted to Islam! From there he fled to a monastery, from which he returned to Granada where he became a respected bookseller, until one day he heard John of Avila preach. From this he suffered (for he certainly did suffer) a conversion. Indeed, he went mad. He was hospitalized in the Hospital Royal de Dementes of Granada, where they tried to beat the devil out of him. He had a hard time living down that hospitalization, but swallowing his pride he became a collector and seller of firewood. Whatever wood was left over he distributed to the poor, "whom he would seek out at night, lying in doorways, freezing and naked, and wounded and sick." He was moved to found his first hospital for their sakes. Years later at the beatification ceremonies, an old woman recalled that a decade after John's death in 1550, young boys would go to the house John had rented and set fire to palm leaves that had been used for wrapping fish, saying, "Juan de Dios used to take the poor up on his shoulders and bring them here to warm them up."

John washed his patients in the public fountain, clothed them minimally, brought them to that house rented with the help of "several devout persons," laid them on litters of bulrushes and covered them with blankets, because that was the only medicine he had to give them. He would go out begging after dark, crying, "Who will do good for himself? " – which became the name of his order in Italy, Fatebenefratelli: "Do good, brethren!" Householders of Granada, at home eating at that hour, brought him their leftovers, which they put into a two-handled basket on his back and two earthenware pots in his hands. Thus he fed his poor and cleaned up after them. A one-man hospital, his first, with many hospital elements in embryo: patient population – the tramps; ward – the naked room; linen supply – the bulrushes; commissary – John, plus the dinners of the neighbors; housekeeping department – John; fundraiser – John.

His second hospital had more of the expected amenities. (There could scarcely have been fewer!) Granada approved of his perseverance and staked him to a larger house, with, it is said, 40 beds. His third hospital, on Gomeles Street in Granada, John left only to die. (Remember, his whole hospital career lasted only nine years, from his age 46 to 55.) In this, as at the very first, care of the soul took precedence over care of the body. Only after the patient confessed did John go out to beg for food. Branching out, he conducted an outpatient service for decent widows and orphans, the "embarrassed poor," higher class females who would rather starve than break seclusion and go out to work. He begged cloth for them to sew clothes for themselves and sell the remainder. Women he rescued he married off, or took them to nurse in his hospital. "The one will marry and the other will say Mass," he remarked in one of his letters.

As so many hospital administrators before and since John's day have discovered, charity has its price. In trying to run a growing hospital with no fixed income on nothing but alms, John was continually short of funds. We have his thoughts on the matter in six surviving letters – dictated; he seems to have been illiterate. With labored initials, "y f o," he signed four of them. The scribe indulged in no capitalization, paragraphing, or punctuation beyond a captious period now and then. Here is John speaking:

so many are the poor who come here that I myself am often astonished that they can be sustained... for counting all sick and healthy and serving people and pilgrims there are over 110 because since this house is general thus people with all illnesses are taken in and people of all kinds thus there are here the lame (in legs and feet) the crippled (in arms and hands) lepers deaf-mutes madmen paralytic the mangy and many other old people and many children and in addition many pilgrims and travelers who arrive here and they are given fire and water and salt and vessels for cooking and for all this there is no income but Jesus Christ will provide for everything for there is no day that there isn't provided for the upkeep of the house four and a half ducats and at times five all this for

bread and meat and chickens and firewood not to mention the medicine and clothing that constitute in themselves an additional expense and on those days when the alms are not sufficient to provide for necessities... I get them on credit and other times they fast.

John owned a vineyard, perhaps the bequest of someone who had died in hospital. For God's sake let it be sold, and quickly too, "in order to pay for meat and oil for they no longer wish to trust me since I owe so much I am holding them off."

very beloved sister of mine the good duchess of sessa send me another ring or anything from your hand so I can pawn it for the other good you sent me has already been used... and all your ladies and damsels should they have some little thing of gold or of silver to send me for the poor and to send to heaven.

today and every day more debts and more poor for there come many naked and barefoot and those with open sores and full of lice we need a man or two to do nothing more than scald lice in a boiling cauldron and this job will last from here on into the winter until the month of may.

I have been so busy around here that I haven't even had time for a slow creed.

John desired to die in his hospital among his poor, but one of his rich patronesses would have none of it. Invoking the principle of obedience, she forced him to remove to her home and suffer luxury in his last days. His body was carried to its grave by every class of citizen of Granada: the poor of the hospital first, then brotherhoods, clergy, municipal council, archbishop, knights and ladies, even the Moorish converts. Realizing they would never see him again, each mourner lunged for the coffin to carry away some memento, "and if God had not seen fit to have them parted from it, they would have torn the coffin to bits, to carry off as relics."

The adventures of John's body persisted beyond the grave. Fifty years after his death his grave was opened, and "the Father Provincial Arias, with great humility and great reverence, took the beads of the blessed father and today carries them with him... And there some of the bones were

divided up among the grave friars who were present... " In 1618 Father Dionysius Celi, prior of the hospital of Juan de Dios of Granada, attempted to buy the bones from the convent where they had been interred, but his hospital was not rich enough to meet the price. So, Celi himself writes,

"Since the blessed body was not intact as they had claimed... Father Friar Dionysius, in the best means and manner that he could, removed from the monastery of Victoria, before his companions and a royal scribe, part of the blessed bones of Father Juan de Dios, which he was given by the one who had them in his possession and was able to give them. These rest today with great veneration in the hospital of Granada..."

What a jewel this body proved to be for John's hospital in

Granada may be inferred from its setting. The interior of the present hospital church (built 1738-39), including its altar, is all the color of gold except the blue interior of its dome. An embossed silver urn in the *camarin* above the altar possibly contains the blessed though partial remains of this "least brother of all the children of God."

One of the earliest offshoots of the hospital in Granada was the one in Lucena (also Andalusia). Founded in 1565, in 1794 it moved into a building still in existence; minimally restored, it may be counted among the least brethren of all the hospitals of John of God. Like so many Spanish hospitals – indeed, like most Spanish homes – it was built around a court, three ward wings at right angles to one another and the church closing the fourth side of the square, entrances to

55   Funerary urn of John of God, church, Hospital de S. Juan de Dios, Granada

56   Hospital de S. Juan de Dios, Lucena, Spain, 18th century

both the wards and the church opening on the street but clearly differentiated architecturally. Though in separate buildings, they follow the general rule: church, ecclesiastical in form; ward, secular. (The court design was inherited from the Arabs, to whom cloistering the womenfolk was of primary importance.)

Hospitals run in families, those of a certain place and time follow a certain philosophy and pattern as hospitals do today. Here is the Hospital de S. Juan de Dios in Antequera (1790). Far grander than the one at Lucena, and larger, it is still the same hospital-church combination, built around an inner court. The bell is to call the nursing community to prayer.

On so many plans of 18th century hospitals there is a section marked: Wood Yard. One only have I seen, that above the chute depositing wood for the stoves in the kitchen of the Hospital de S. Juan de Dios, Jaen (also Andalusia). The wood was not split logs, but twisty, knotted stumps.

57   The fountain in the center of the court, Hospital de S. Juan de Dios, Lucena

60   Wood yard, Hospital de S. Juan de Dios, Jaen, Spain

61   Not a fireplace, but a chute for stove wood. Kitchen, Hospital de S. Juan de Dios, Jaen, Spain

58   A very smelly sink in one of the wards, Hospital de S. Juan de Dios, Lucena

59   Court, looking toward ward buildings, Hospital de S. Juan de Dios, Antequera, Spain, 1790

5 CROSS-SHAPED HOSPITALS

The cross-shaped hospital was declared in 1781 to be "the usual form of hospitals in many Roman-Catholic countries." John Howard, the British philanthropist, who made this statement, had visited more European hospitals than any man of his day.

The cross shape was of course of great symbolic value. But the primary reason for its widespread adoption was not symbolic or mystical. Unexpectedly, it was utilitarian, a matter of simple efficiency. If the chapel of a hospital is placed at the crossing, four times as many patients could see, or at least hear, the Mass.

At the Ospedale di Santo Spirito, Rome, three wards led off in three of the four directions from an elaborate central altar. One of the wards is depicted in a 17th century print, showing not only two rows against the side walls of the canopied beds properly belonging to this ward, but also four rows of pallets on the floor between them – presumably an instance of overcrowding in time of pestilence. For three centuries that organ on the left wall played for the sick three times a day. An anonymous 17th century English report describes this hospital:

"When you come in you shall see right out before, on both sides, three hundred beds standing, all hung with very fair curtains, the bedsteads carved, nightgowns, pantables, and other necessaries in order placed by every bed. So soon as a sick body comes thither (for none are refused) he is set on a bench, until the doctors and surgeons are brought to him, with the apothecaries, by whom the sick are visited. He is presently accepted, his bedding appointed, and immediately a clean sweet shirt is given him. His cloaths are laid up, till he recovers, or dies... Both sides are hung with arras in winter-time, in summer with gilded leather, from the ground to the top. There are continually found at this hospital, above three thousand persons, as, children, nurses, widows, and other poor people, that are there maintained..."

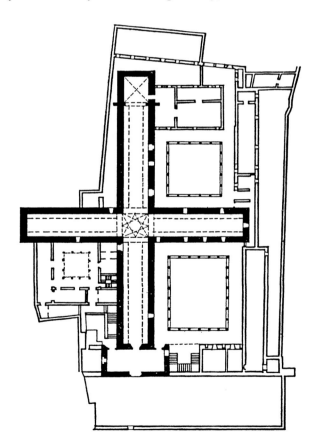

62   Cross-shaped hospital plan: one chapel at the crossing and a second at the top. Hospital de Santa Cruz, Toledo, Spain, 1514

63   Sistina ward as seen from the central chapel, Ospedale di Santo Spirito, Rome, a 17th century print

*prospectus mediæ partis maio[...]
aulæ Nosocomij*

In 1966 the two wards to either side of the chapel, after lying empty for many years, had been restored and patients were assigned to them again. This is the way the larger ward looked from a small viewing window in the administrator's apartment (in the 17th century print, first panel on the left in the narrow rear wall, up near the ceiling). The archway to the great golden altar had been glassed in against drafts. You are looking down on the Sistina ward, at this time used for women.

The smaller ward, for men, is shown from ground level. The doctors cussed at the practice of medicine in such wards and assigned to them only their lightest cases. Portable screens required for privacy at times in such a setting can be seen at intervals down the walls. By the time ten years had elapsed the historic wards were once again emptied of patients.

65   Men's ward, Santo Spirito, Rome

64   Sistina Ward, Ospedale di Santo Spirito, 1966

Here is the chapel of the 18th century Old Age Home in Arbois, Burgundy. Without stirring the curtains one knows what lies behind them. There was a similar arch on the opposite side of the chapel. The effectiveness of the Arbois chapel is thus doubled. A number of 18th century hospitals in the area employed a similar construction.

66   Chapel, Old Age Home, Arbois, France, 18th century

67   Behind the chapel curtain, Old Age Home, Arbois, France

A very small – perhaps the very smallest – cross-shaped hospital is the Hôtel-Dieu of Gray, in Burgundy, France (early 18th century). All four arms can be seen at once from the rear of the building, the fourth as a cross over the entrance. Under that dome at the crossing is of course a chapel.

68   Hôtel-Dieu, Gray, Burgundy, France, 18th century

The rest of this chapter will *very properly* (as John Howard liked to say) be devoted to the Ospedale Maggiore of Milan. It was the first cross ward to be conceived as a whole (by Filarete, architect to the Duke of Milan, in 1456) and as such immensely influential. Imitations based on the plans alone sprang up within 50 years.

Here a plan is indispensable. The Ospedale Maggiore was projected as two crosses of great size, one on the right of a central courtyard for men and one on the left for women. That for men was completed in the first spurt of building, the one for women not for 350 years. Meanwhile women were tucked into an arm of the men's ward. The central courtyard, achieved only by degrees, had a church at its head opposite the entrance. Our plan dates from the 18th century, when the second cross was finally completed in a style of architecture undreamed-of by Filarete. It shows how smaller courts were formed by inscribing the cross wards within service rooms. Each court was devoted to a different function.

The open wards, two storeys in height, were taller than the two-storeyed service rooms surrounding them, while the roof of the chapel at the crossing was taller still. The photograph across one of the four small courts was taken after a direct bomb hit during World War II had made the complex look like a ruin, and before restoration would transform this hospital into the campus of the University of Milan.

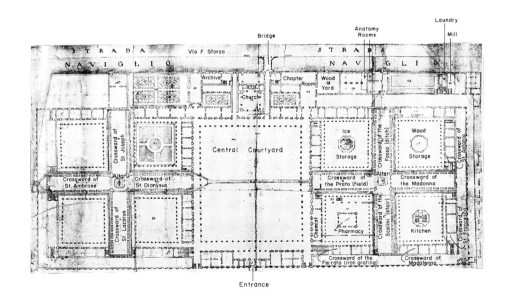

69   Plan of the Ospedale Maggiore, Milan Italy, 1456

70   Courtyard, looking toward chapel at crossing, Ospedale Maggiore,
      Milan

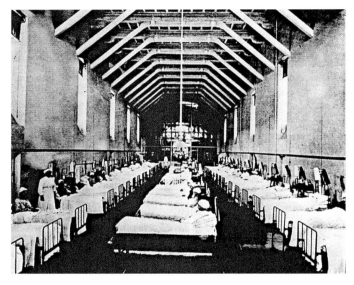

In 1966 the cross ward of the Prato was gutted even of the beams that supported its ceiling when it had patients in it. The chapel at the crossing, as an old photograph shows, was glassed in as at Rome. This space has since become the library of the University of Milan.

The cross wards were elevated by a full basement, itself half above ground, with light coming from the sides, cross ventilation, and walls thick enough for a fortress. It was never used for patients, but wine and bread were made

72 Cross ward of the Prato in 1966, Ospedale Maggiore, Milan

73 Cross ward of the Prato earlier, with patients in it, Ospedale Maggiore

71 Basement, cross ward, Ospedale Maggiore, Milan

66

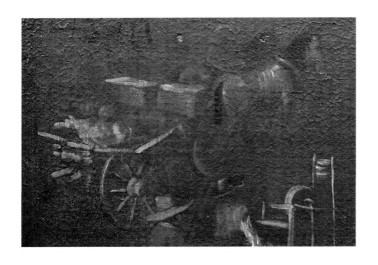

down there, the laundresses worked there, and meat for the patients was brought in on the hoof and slaughtered at need in one of the basement rooms. Hens were raised in the women's ward.

The details of a late 17th century painting show live meat being brought to the hospital, and a patient (hopefully alive) similarly delivered. The ambulance is distinguished by a little bell.

The key to this picture is the bestowal of alms. Once a year, on the Festa del Perdono, all Milan flocked to the Ospedale Maggiore, where to give alms meant the pardoning of sins, the saving of one's soul, and - for the hospital - remaining solvent one more year.

75   The patient ambulance, Ospedale Maggiore, Milan

74   Delivery of meat on the hoof. Ospedale Maggiore, Milan

76   Almsgiving on the Festa del Perdono, Ospedale Maggiore, Milan

Brotherhoods and trade guilds attended, each as a corporate body. Here is the apothecary guild, its leader proudly flourishing a clyster (enema), badge of the trade.

Having conveniently removed the wall toward the courtyard of the Cross Ward of the Prato, the late 17th century artist shows a scene of last rites within, and, one pillar further on, what seems in a shadowy way to be an interment. Well might it remain shadowy! Imagination boggles at the original burial arrangements of the Ospedale Maggiore. Filarete spelled it out clearly: he would have an upper altar in the church of the central courtyard, at the head of the plan, and a lower altar in the church vault.

"Above the ground," he writes, "there are four columns where a Mass is said every Monday for the souls of the dead. Below the altar one can go down by this stair to the very bottom. It has several openings above for putting in bodies." Filarete describes "parallel iron bars, like a grating, where the bodies are laid. This is almost at the level of the water." It will be seen on the plan that right behind the church ran the Naviglio, the town canal. Filarete was counting on it heavily. Professor Robert Herrlinger was once asked what services in such a church would be like, as the smell wafted upward, and he replied, "I fear that the problem how to do away with the corpses was much more important than the problem how to do away with the smell!"

But eventually the smell daunted everybody. One reads of overflowing vaults, an accumulation of corpses 50 yards from the infirmary that saturated the ground, common trenches into which the naked dead were thrown in time of pestilence, the remains eventually treated with unslaked lime. There was even a desperate suggestion by the Tribunal of *Health* to unstop the sepulchers toward the Naviglio and let them drain into the city canal! In 1694 a new burial ground was opened well beyond the city limits.

77   The Apothecary Guild on the Festa del Perdono, Ospedale Maggiore, Milan

78   Deathbed, Festa del Perdono, Ospedale Maggiore

Here we see a funeral headed across the central courtyard - headed rearward, which means this was a pauper who had died. Wealthy deceased left in state by the principal portal. Paupers were taken by a back door over a little bridge across the Naviglio, that came to be known as the "Bridge of the Poor."

Ward accommodations were likewise separate and unequal. The poor, as ever, got the open wards. But in 1685 an English traveler reported of the Ospedale Maggiore:

"In this hospital there are not only Galleries full of Beds on both sides, as is ordinary in all Hospitals; but there are also a great many Chambers in which persons whose condition was formerly distinguished are treated with a particular care."

79   Funeral, Ospedale Maggiore

One can pick out smaller wards on the plan in the encircling (or ensquaring) service wings. They were for rich strangers, who paid; for the Embarrassed Poor; for Decayed Gentlefolk. Rich Milanese as usual were nursed at home.

It would require a whole book to describe all that is going on at the late 17th century celebration of the Festa del Perdono in the great courtyard of the Ospedale Maggiore of Milan, but here is a photograph of the painting as a whole.

80   The courtyard painting, Festa del Perdono, Ospedale Maggiore,
      Milan, 17th century

So impressive did this hospital seem to contemporaries over a period of three hundred years - until, in the 18th century, Italy became too poor to maintain its charitable standards - that another 17th century British traveler has this to say:

"The great hospital built in a quadrangle upon arches and round pillars is a most magnificent thing. Really if sickness were not a little unwholesome and troublesome, a man would almost wish to be a little sick here, where a King, though in health, might lodge handsomely."

The terra-cotta window is one among many, individually decorated, that adorn the central section of the façade of the Ospedale Maggiore which closes in the central court from the street. Both court and façade were made possible by a very rich man, a banker and dealer in wool. This suggests two paradoxes. First, the money was converted into ornate architectural reality at a very bad time for the hospital and for Milan - a time of plague. Second, donor and architect alike were thinking in palace terms for a hospital for paupers. The second paradox is almost a platitude, it happened so often. Filarete, the hospital's first architect, expressed at the outset the palace way of thinking:

"Magnanimous and great princes, and republics as well, should not hold back from building great and beautiful buildings because of the expense. No country was ever made poor nor did anyone ever die because of the construction of buildings... In the end, when a large building is completed, there is neither more nor less money in the country, but the building does remain in the country or the city together with its reputation and honor."

81   One window, Ospedale Maggiore, Milan

PART TWO
TYPES OF HOSPITALS

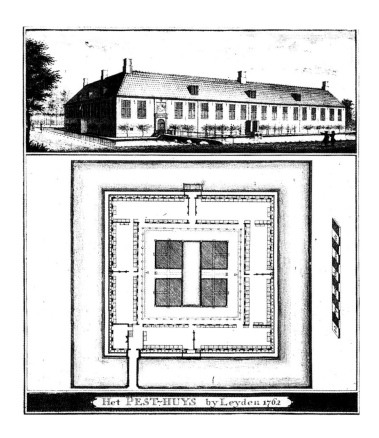

99   Plan of Pest House, Leiden, begun 1635

6 THE HOUSING OF CONTAGION

....*Behold, if the rising of the sore be white reddish in his bald head, or in his bald forehead, as the leprosy appeareth in the skin of the flesh;*

He is a leprous man, he is unclean: the priest shall pronounce him utterly unclean; his plague is in his head.

And the leper in whom the plague is, his clothes shall be rent, and his head bare, and he shall put a covering upon his upper lip, and shall cry, Unclean, unclean.

All the days wherein the plague shall be in him he shall be defiled; he is unclean; he shall dwell alone; without the camp shall his habitation be.

Leviticus 13:43-46

82   The leper with his clapper, and the dogs lick his sores. Hospital San Lazaro, Seville

It is now generally believed that the disease called *zaarat* in Leviticus and translated "leprosy" was a skin infection or cluster of infections unrelated to the leprosy of the Middle Ages – save that the passage in Leviticus gave Europeans a notion of how to deal with what they were faced with, true leprosy or Hansen's Disease, named for the man who discovered the bacillus in 1874. This disease had been reported in France as early as 640 A.D. It was so horrible, people pretended it wasn't there as long as they could. True leprosy is a loathsome disease, though nowhere near as contagious as it was thought to be in the Middle Ages. Besides the skin lesions, it can cause a foul breath, great irritability, deteriorating extremities, and a fearful sexual appetite. Only a Christian saint could welcome lepers, kiss their rotting feet or empty eye sockets, and call them "jewels." For ordinary mortals it is probable that fear of contagion was secondary to physical revulsion. By the 12th century leprosy had reached epidemic proportions and action had to be taken. The action was that recommended by Leviticus. Lepers were expelled and leprosaria built.

A leprosarium was walled in. It might be built as a ward-chapel arrangement or as a collection of houses, resembling a little town. It was likely to be a row of single, yet attached, dwellings in some relationship to a central church, much like a Charterhouse of religious recluses, sharing a cloister.

St. George's leprosarium, in Stettin, Poland (16th Century) is the paradigm: outside the town gates, but on a main road, with a sentry-box for the representative of the community who proffered the almsbox. Like monks, the lepers might elect one of themselves to be their master – Charles Mercier calls the leprosarium a combined monastery, prison, and

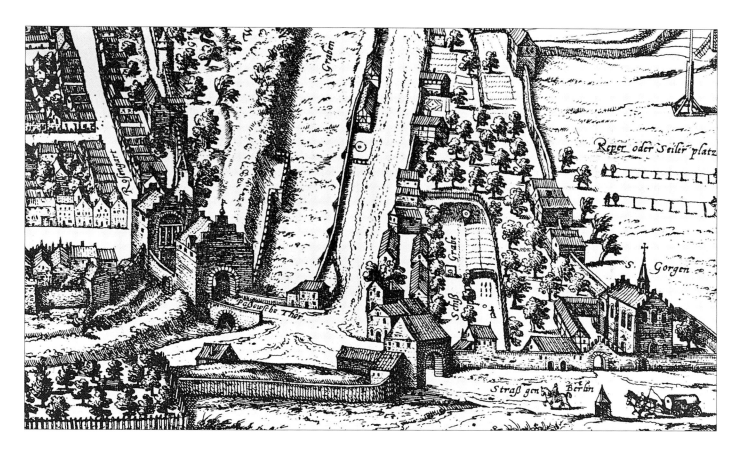

almshouse. Prison: the plan of the leper hospital of St. Giles, London, shows a gallows at the entrance. To quote Mercier again:

"At Greenside in Scotland, if any leper lay out the night the offence was a hanging matter, and lest any leper should plead that he knew not, or had forgotten the penalty, the authorities thoughtfully set up a gibbet before the gate of the hospital to remind him."

83   St. George's Leprosarium, Stettin, Poland, 16th Century

Yet a leper house might live so well on alms that paupers were known to feign leprosy to gain admittance, and sometimes the premises were raided or annexed by the envious. The sexes were expected to live segregated from one another as in a religious house, and that was difficult to accept – after all, these lepers, unlike monks or nuns, had not elected to live celibate! Social distinctions were not totally obliterated – at Dauphigné there was one leper house for common folk, another for nobles, and a third for Ladies of the Court.

Though there were so many medieval leprosaria – 2,000 in France in 1226, with about 220 in England and Scotland – few have survived. With the loss of patients, many reverted to farms (which is what, after all, they had been, for lepers had been the farmers). This is what happened to the leprosarium of Meursault, near Beaune, France, founded before 1142. The central church, now used as a barn, can clearly be discerned, and the sentry box is just left of its main door. That door has been walled up and the rear entrance to the sentry box as well.

Of interest is the alms slot, here stuffed with a newspaper. It is narrow outside the wall, and opens wide within. At right angles to this was a range of individual dwellings, their suviving doorways all but hidden by chicken coops.

84   Sentry door, Meursault

85   Alms slot from outside, Meursault

87   Alms slot from inside, Meursault

86   Leprosarium, Meursault, 12th century

One last lonely symbol of the exclusion of the leper: the point of this picture of an altar in a church in Copenhagen is the dark oblong hole in the wall. It led to an opening on the street at ear level round which lepers might congregate to hear Mass.

88   Hole for the lepers to hear Mass, Copenhagen

Cerusico, Medico, e Confes.sporchi. 31. Carrette, e Profumatori sporchi, che profu...
le robbe, che mandano allo spurgo. 35. Carretoni, che portano via le dette robbe.

Both leprosy and plague were perceived as contagious, but plague was swift. There was no time for loathing. Rather there was fear. Lepers were banished to live in leprosaria in the fields. Plague victims might be expelled to the fields to die, and few dared come near, even to offer a cup of water to the dying, or to bury the dead. Doctors and clergy were often the first to flee.

In Italy the plague watch was organized to the hilt, from town to town. Each town had its Magistrate for Health. Messengers constantly reported the spread of the infection. Travel was prohibited from town to town – ordinary travel, that is; important people, such as ambassadors, and their entourage, even from areas known to be infected, were greeted ceremonially at the city gates. How socially unequal the conception of infection was is shown in four broadsides of the plague in Rome in 1656. Goods were ordered to be destroyed if from an infected house – or disinfected, depending on their value. Here is the house of a poor man, where the law is being carried out to the letter. Episode #31 is labeled, "Contaminated carts, and fumigators, who fumigate the houses and burn the rubbish." The key word here is "rubbish." It was of little value, it only belonged to a poor man.

89   Burning the poor man's infected goods. The Plague at Rome, 1656

8. Modo di profumare libri, e Scritture dalli sporchi. 9. Assistenza del Religioso sporco, e Commiss.º polito, mentre trouano nele Case gioie, danari, et altro.

This was the house of a rich man, a fire of another sort! While the owner is being borne out to the cart for the dead, gold is being weighed out by bare hand right in front of the body. Books are being brought out to be fumigated. The work is supervised by a "contaminated" religious (#9) and (back to back) a "contaminated" commissioner – those who worked with the dead were considered contaminated and had to wear some identifying sign, usually a white stole, which one sees on the commissioner. The caption reads:

"Meanwhile they find jewels, money, and other things in the house."

An extremely valuable commodity was clothing – of the rich, of course. This was carefully loaded on carts and taken to a vineyard where each item was carefully sunned and aired along the vines. In Palermo in 1575 a commercial disinfection establishment was opened in the vegetable garden, orchard, and rabbit run of the Duke of Bilbona. Rabbit

90   Disposing of the rich man's infected goods. The Plague at Rome, 1656

91   Disinfection grounds, Palermo, Sicily, 1575

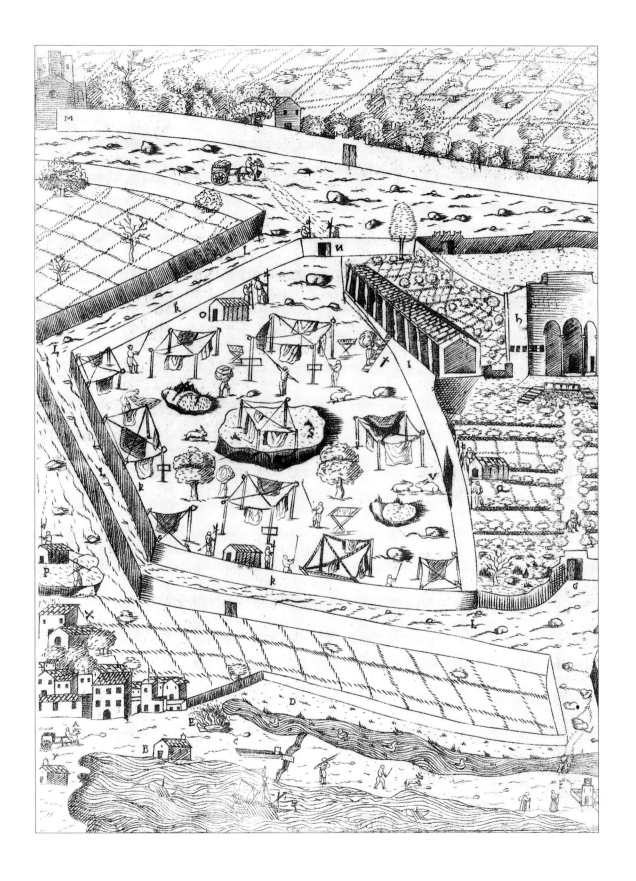

run: Italians keep and use rabbits as we would chickens. The Duke himself took in patients in a one-storey lazaretto built in the shape of a hollow square right at the foot of the towering Ducal palace.

Each square pictured represents one family's belongings. Proportions here are way off; there are said to have been a hundred or more airing spaces each at least 24 feet square, set 40 feet apart. The site is guarded by four men with halberds. In bad weather the goods were taken down and stored at the rear right in a row of rooms reached by ladder, each family's belongings in a carefully marked bundle. They might be cleaned with lye, soapsuds, or in the case of silk pure water, "but it would be better to cleanse them by wind, sun and bright weather, and with scents." All this for 30 days. The workers, men and women, were seen as putting their lives in jeopardy; they must confess, be bled, be very highly paid – and utterly trustworthy.

At the bottom of our picture is a village for convalescents, shown walking with a stick because of buboes at the thigh.

In spite of all this, and the hanging, burning, decapitation and quartering of those who ran away, the cities of Italy were still unable to halt the plague. Each building converted for use as a lazaretto in Rome in 1656 had a gallows at its front door – but that did not prevent plague victims from breaking bounds.

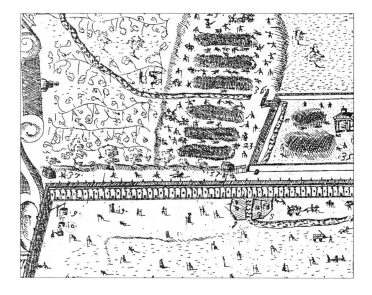

92   Burial trenches, Lazaretto, Milan, 1631

The Lazaretto of the Ospedale Maggiore of Milan was purpose-built from a plan of 1488; our etching shows how it looked in 1631. Some might say the location was entirely too close to the city – a stone's throw outside the city walls, in fact, but the donor who gave the land specified that site and no other.

It was believed that wind would blow contagion into the city.

Answer: The city is to the southwest of the lazaretto, so the wind would not be the bad west wind which putrefies, but the good north, east, or south winds which are healthful. "Besides, if there really were such a danger...it would exist even if the distance were a thousand paces, because of how fast the wind moves." (Luca Beltrami, *Il Lazaretto di Milano, 1488-1882,* Milan, 1899, p.22).

It was thought that noxious exhalations would escape cityward from the patient rooms.

Answer: "Most exhalations remain in the rooms anyway, and if any small amounts escape through the window they are immediately counteracted by the warmth of the sun in daylight or by the stars at night through the mediation of the rays mixed in with the air."

There were 288 contiguous rooms arranged around an enormous court. Each side of the hollow square was five hundred yards long. There was a continuous arcaded walkway before the doors on three sides, with only two doors out of the enclosure, one toward the town at the bottom of the drawing, and one toward the mass burial pits at the rear (#29). Each room was to hold eight patients, with one privy whose drain vented into a moat that completely surrounded the lazaretto with water. No rushing stream, this; though the ditch of the moat was 15 feet wide on top, water flowed only at its narrow bottom, and the privy vents opened just above the water. And yet this water was considered "clean" – uninfected, as clean as any other open sewer! The "unclean" water-course was the one draining the laundry (#5) on this "truthful representation with correct measurements of the great lazaretto... as it was at the time of the great pestilence, 1631," by Francesco Brunetti.

93   Etching of the Lazaretto of Milan in time of plague, 1631

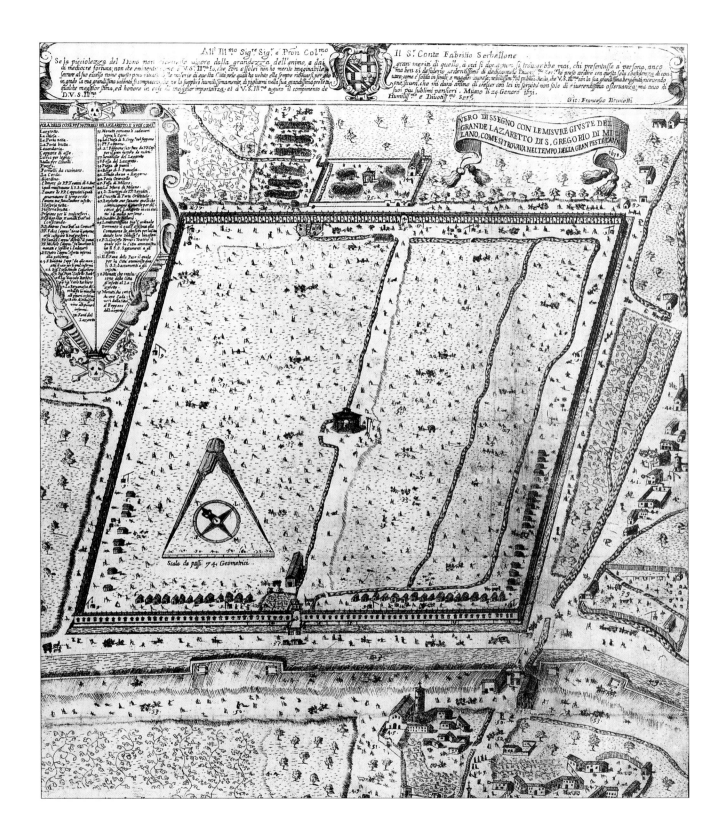

"There must be a double water, one will be the water of the surrounding ditch... which will be clean, and if this water were to flow into... another ditch it will do no harm... The other water must be that in which the clothes of the sick are washed, as well as their soil, and this... must have an outlet through some other channel so that in no way can it flow in the direction of the city." On the etching detail one sees the water flowing through the laundry at #5, under the moat and the street beyond it, through the graveyard of the church of St. Gregory, past the original mass graves, here grassed over (#35), past the first three trenches, surrounded by stick figures with shovels, and already three more mass graves have been dug (some of the stick figures are lying down, they are to be buried) and a fourth one is being frantically started. A time of pestilence indeed! Thence the sewer heads off away from the city.

Drinking water came from wells spaced at regular intervals, four on the left and four on the right sides of the square, and two top and bottom, all numbered 9; one can be seen in the upper left on the detail, within the court.

So much for sanitation, now for the church. Octagonal, in the very center of the huge court, it had almost no external walls: "a building as it were in filigree," wrote Manzoni, who set in this lazaretto major episodes of his best-selling novel, *I Promessi Sposi, The Betrothed*. Like the church at the crossing of a cross ward, it was intended to give every patient a view of the Mass from his or her room.

The church was later encased in solid walls. A photograph from 1882, when the patient rooms had been turned into shops and the moat was filled in, best conveys, however, the size of this institution. The octagonal church can be seen to the rear, in front of a railroad trestle that crosses the site, at the halfway point of the huge square. The far range of the Lazaretto can be dimly made out in the distance beyond it.

Looking back from the 19th century, Manzoni claims that during the plague of 1631, which this etching depicts, ten thousand people thronged the Lazaretto enclosure. He describes it as completely cluttered with cabins and sheds. In the accompanying detail the huts are beginning to rise to the right of the clean door, within the wall that faced Milan. Women and children, says Manzoni, were kept apart in a tract of cabins behind a kind of palisade fence. An alley was cleared from clean door to dirty door, past the church.

There was neither time nor money to decorate a structure designed for such use, and overuse. The builders were idealistic and projected that under the portico, a large niche be set into the outer wall of each room, with a painting to identify it: "Outside the first room Almighty God, outside the second room etc. etc. And from one room to the next there will be one depiction after another to the very last room." Not one was even started.

95   The central church, Lazaretto, Milan   94   Lazaretto, Milan, 1882

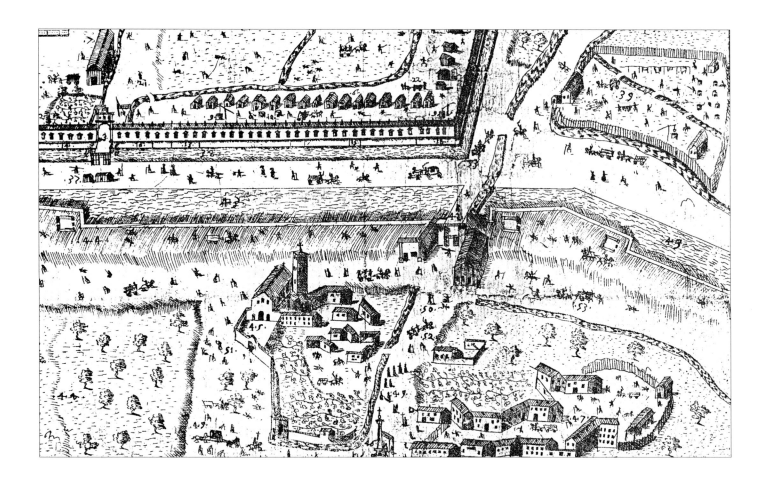

Next to the church, in the center of the etching, is a gallows with its victim. #32 is described as "maid servants of the Lazaretto." #21 is labeled, "Father Felice, Capucin, castigates transgressors." Presumably the maid servants were brought to watch and learn. This little world had more than its share of crime; deadbeats who could function under such conditions had little fear of consequences. There was a jail at the lower right-hand corner of the great square, and it was needed.

Identifications in this enlarged section of the plan shed light on some of the workers in this plague hospital. At #19, Father Zumelli, Theatine, is seen with a big cross hurrying to take confession; in the picture as a whole there are two #19s, heading opposite ways. #33, the *monati* were something more than gravediggers: seen here with their cart,

they collected bodies, and they led the sick to their destination – a dirty job. In two places #24, a Capucin, "exhorts the sick to be patient."

The patient being addressed is ambulatory, as shown by the two staffs. Perhaps he or she will live to be discharged. The enclave seen just inside the walls of Milan in the previous picture was the convalescent area, "Paradise." After 20 days in Paradise, patients were discharged to their homes, where for another 15 days they were supervised and subjected to careful washings and perfumings.

This strange cartoon-like record even describes dietary arrangements. At five places, all adjacent to the arcade and evenly spaced, it shows outdoor double cooking ovens. At #30 (in two places), "the woman from Bergamo distributes soup to the poor sick" – two women carry the soup pot between them. At #31, "Batista distributes the wine." #22 (two places), a Capucin distributes bread from a horse-or mule-driven cart.

In 1576, each sick person received daily four ordinary loaves of bread, three large glasses of wine mixed with water, one pound of meat, and two ladles of soup (minestrone).For those recovering the allowance was less ample: three loaves of bread, two cups of wine, one ladle of soup, four ounces of meat; and for women and children even less: only two loaves of bread and one and a half glasses of wine, otherwise the same. Cheese instead of meat on Friday and Saturday.

A medical presence is slightly indicated at #29. This is one of the three barber-surgeons. Let the names be recorded: Signor Francesco Castello, Signor Giacinto, and Signor Cario. Physicians and lawyers would not risk their learning or their lives by entering the enclosure of the Lazaretto of St. Gregory. They stood across the 15-foot moat and shouted prescriptions to the patient standing at the window, or took wills. The barbers entered among the sick, lived with them, and lanced their boils – one of the few procedures, if not the only one, that brought some relief.

The Milan architectural solution for a pest house was widely adopted. In 1635 a Pest House was begun at Leiden in the Netherlands, in the form of a hollow square surrounded by water, with but a single entrance by bridge. (For the single bridge at the front entrance of the Milan Lazaretto, a drawbridge had been suggested!) Drains crisscrossed the court underground, emptying into the moat.

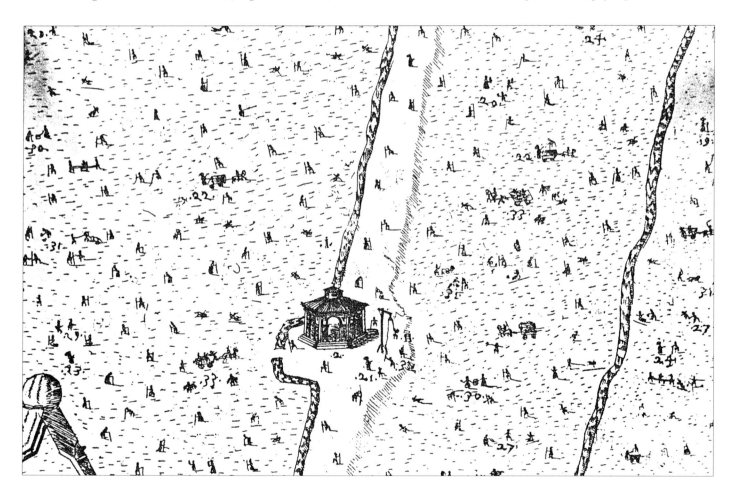

97   The central church, Lazaretto, Milan

98   Pest House, Leiden: front entrance, and the single bridge over the moat that surrounds it on all four sides, filled with water.

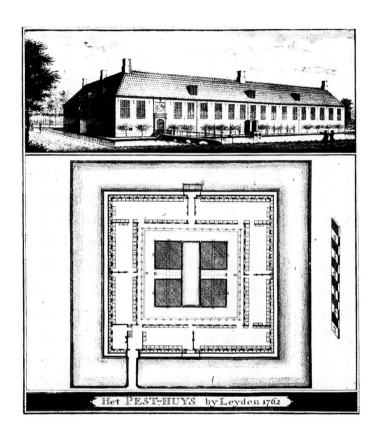

Het PEST-HUYS by Leyden 1762

The Pest House is on an infinitely smaller scale than the Lazaretto of Milan. There were two wards to a side, intended for multiple occupancy. The plan shows 22 to 31 beds in each. No chapel is shown in the court or any place else. Nowadays the building is used as a military museum.

99   Plan of Pest House, Leiden, begun 1635

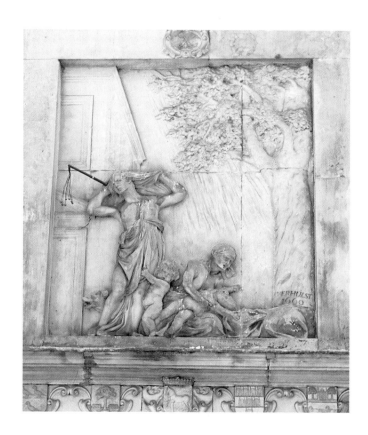

The scourge of the plague: a dead child, a grieving grand-
mother, a mother stricken by plague with her remaining
child clinging to her, and a whip, a real metal scourge, jut-
ting out from the bas relief.

100   The Scourge of the Plague. Bas relief, front door, Pest House, Leiden,
      1660

7 ON PRIVIES AND HOUSEKEEPING

Thus far, a good deal has been said about chapels, but nothing at all about privies. However motivated by matters of the spirit a hospital staff might be, they had to deal with bodies on a daily basis. Indeed, an historic hospital staff might be thought of as suspended at equal distance between chapel and privy.

At the Ospedale Maggiore of Milan, privy provisions were generous and complicated. Between every two beds of the open cross wards was a door leading to a privy – some of these doors can still be seen in the old photograph of the ward in use. Three modern beds fit in the space occupied by one 15th century bed (which we may think of as similar to the bed in the church in Pistoia, with a chest at the foot for the patient's belongings). A floor plan by Hansgeorg Knoblauch reconstructs the original setup.

On this photograph of the privy corridor the seat level of one cubicle has been removed, revealing the curved upper arch of the passage for the open drain below.

Filarete was very proud of his sanitary innovation. Water from the Naviglio, the canal, was diverted at A on the diagram, to be led either by immediate detour to B, the laundry, and thence back under the canal to the open fields beyond; or, regulated by a series of sluices, it swept under

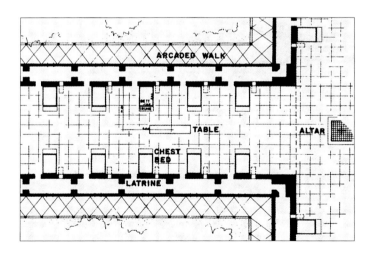

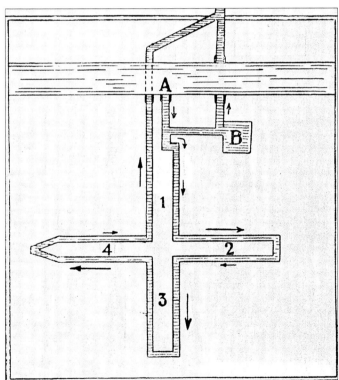

102   Filarete's privy system, Ospedale Maggiore

101   One arm of the cross ward showing privy arrangement. Ospedale Maggiore, Milan

103   Privy corridor from seat level, drain beneath. Ospedale Maggiore, Milan

the privy corridors of arms 1, 2, 3, and 4 of the great cross ward building, following the direction of the arrows. Conducted under the Naviglio and thereafter let loose, "it cleans the latrines and the road outside the city to the great advantage of anyone who owns fields in that direction." Some hospitals sold their organic wastes.

Filarete proposed to do away with every last vestige of odor by spiracles every ten *braccia* (a *braccio* is 22 inches) rising through the buttresses to the roof. The spiracles were supposed to work both ways: in dry weather bad air was to rise *up* them, in a rainfall they were to be rinsed by pure rainwater pouring *down* them.

By 1695 (239 years after its installation!) only the intake of the privy system was in working order.

The granddaddy of all drains was the monastic necessarium. This is the sewer of the dormitory necessarium at Kirkstall Abbey, England. The arch and sill of the entrance door from dormitory to seats (now of course vanished) can be seen at the left.

104 Privy drain, Kirkstall Abbey, England

A unique glimpse into an 18th century hospital necessarium does not specify seating but does suggest heating (chimney and fireplace at left). This was in the basement of Guy's Hospital, London, 1725.

The privy of the large open ward that was St. John's Hospital, Bruges, was in the very midst of the ward – it is that white boxy structure center rear in the oil painting by Johannes Beerblock, "View of the Sick Ward of St. John's Hospital, 1778." This painting gives us a great deal of other information about late 18th century European hospitals. Let us enter it by the privy door (or doors – there would be one for each sex, since this ward is divided by sex right down the middle) and ask ourselves, Why is a necessary house in the middle of the ward?

Then there was the dry privy, not flushed by a stream and requiring periodic emptying. "Night soil men" proudly performed their periodic task by the light of the moon, according to a picture at the heading of a bill for work done at one of the houses owned by the Hospital of St. Bartholomew, London, January 26, 1757 (2 tons) and September 13, 1757 (8 tons), at a cost of £2.

106   Privies, Guy's Hospital, London, 1725

107   (overleaf) Johannes Beerblock, "View of the Sick Ward of St. John's Hospital, 1778," Bruges, Belgium

105   "Night soil men," St. Bartholomew's Hospital, 18th century

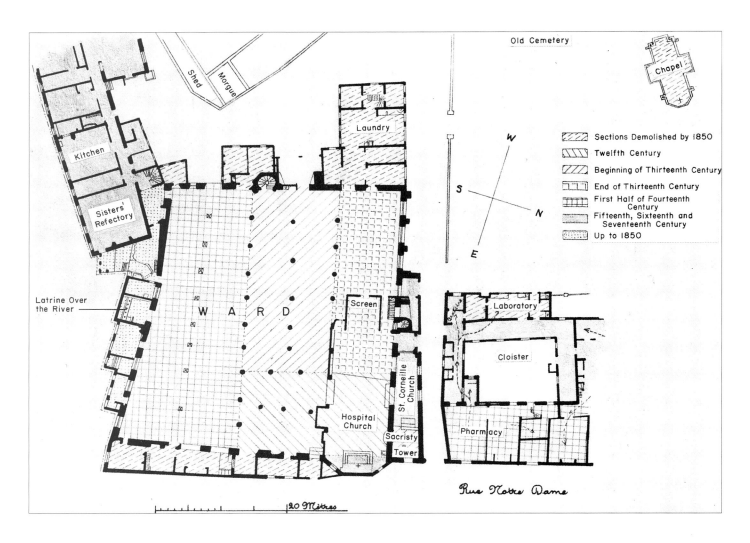

Legend:
- Sections Demolished by 1850
- Twelfth Century
- Beginning of Thirteenth Century
- End of Thirteenth Century
- First Half of Fourteenth Century
- Fifteenth, Sixteenth and Seventeenth Century
- Up to 1850

Unlike the Hospices Civils of Strasbourg, St. John's Hospital did its growing on one site and its stages of growth can be shown on one floor plan. First (lines slanting down from the left) there was only the corner church and the area south of it: a ward-chapel combination, along rue Notre Dame. There would have been privies behind that 12th century ward, flushed by a diverted arm of the River Reie (left margin of the plan; latrines over the river are an 18th century addition).

At the beginning of the 13th century the ward expanded westward from the church (broken squares). At the end of the 13th century an addition (lines slanting up from the left) completed the ward as a large oblong with privies still outside. In the first half of the 14th century, with Bruges at the peak of its power and influence, the ward expanded southward clear to the river, enclosing the original privies in a structure of their own. In a later painting of the interior of this ward, several bunk beds had been removed at the end of the row next to the privies, for understandable reasons.

A few years ago a movie company using the old hospital as a stage set manufactured fog over the river, which entered the original drain and came up through a small vent in the ward floor just where the white boxy structure once stood.

108 Floor plan showing expansion, St. John's Hospital, Bruges, Belgium

To paint his picture of the ward in action, Beerblock set up his easel in front of the circular staircase to the attic or, even more likely, considering his width and angle of view, part way up the stair looking out through an opening that is still there.

What these stages of building add up to in terms of variegated window and roof levels one sees on the south facade of the old hospital, along the River Reie. The 14th century ward is in the right foreground, the latrines added later are that first low projection to the right. Behind the ward and at an angle to it is a 17th century convent for the Augustinian nuns who nursed in this hospital.

109   South façade, St. John's Hospital, Bruges, Belgium

Here is the northern façade of the St. John's Hospital, as seen in 1965 from approximately the center of the compass rose on the floor plan.

To return to our starting place: the indoor privy. A pipe sweeps upward from the ceiling of the little white boxy structure, no doubt to vent above the building roof. Just in front of the privy, four people are engaged in a very familiar hospital activity: solicitation of alms. Two portly bishops (to judge by their rings) and a sister who in this context must be the Mother Superior represent St. John's "Big Gifts Division" in action. They solicit a gentleman of the world, with sword and laces. One bishop extends the begging cup, his eyes discreetly averted. The other, hand on heart, with a great flourish indicates the work of charity of this hospital. The choice of cubicle is questionable, for in the very next one he will find a female patient standing on a mattress, feeding her leftovers to a cat. In the background, with reassuring pat, a nurse sends off a departing relative or cured patient; behind them a patient lifts himself from bed by the cord slung for that purpose across all cubicles and beds.

111   Solicitation of alms, Beerblock painting

110   North façade, St. John's Hospital, Bruges, Belgium

112   Feeding the cat, Beerblock painting

"Turn it and turn it, everything is in it" (a Talmudic saying). Beerblock's genre painting shows the hospital ward in full action – livelier indeed than at any one given time of the day or night. He has packed in every conceivable activity save the resurrection of the dead. And all going on at the same time. The aisle left of center terminated at the rear of the chapel, which was then open to the ward (and since walled in). Monuments, plaques and statues glitter on the chapel walls. Toward it, as far back into this aisle as we can see, a corpse is being carried. A convalescent, in red robe and the kind of bedcap worn by many male patients here, weaves down the aisle; a nurse arrives through the aisle between cupboard beds with a tray of medications; drink is being poured from a large jar – probably beer, since the water was usually undrinkable; probably fairly small beer.

Note that a cupboard bed could be converted to a crib bed for an unconscious patient.

In the most prominent position at the head of this aisle a curé administers Last Rites. This would be Father G. Kinjedt, the administrator, who commissioned this painting. The patient is making a good death. He smiles as though already he felt "through all this fleshly dress Bright shoots of ever-lastingness." The curé holds a plant, hyssop – he is sprinkling the dying man with holy water.

113   Left aisle, rear, Beerblock painting   114   Extreme unction, Beerblock painting

Which would explain the square of red at the left front corner of the table at which the nun is kneeling: hyssop would deteriorate if it were stored in the holy water, so it was left to dry on a red cloth. (These identifications were made by Professor Stephan Kuttner.) The altar table seems to be an ordinary ward table decked for the purpose with ornate cloths. We can make out an open prayerbook; a ciborium in which the wafers of the sacrament were kept; a large key with red tassel – far too big for the ciborium, probably belonging to the chapel cabinet where it was stored; a crucifix with slim arms and sturdy base; and two mismatched candlesticks, one brass, one pewter. The nursing sister holds a third long candle in her hand and in her other hand the curl of burning paper with which she lit it. On the footboard of the bed behind the table stands a pitcher with a towel thrown over it, used by Father Kinjedt for a ceremonial washing of hands before officiating. In front of this

table is an ordinary box, with a tasseled crimson pillow for kneeling. How these brightly-coloured trappings must have traveled about the ward! Behind the table, in the center of the aisle, is the bed, well-made and ready, into which the patient will be moved to die.

That such was the custom in this hospital is clear from the deathbed scene in the middle aisle, at the center of the painting. The patient has received the final sacrament, nothing to do now but pray for her. Her table is bare, except for a hospital metal dish, pitcher, spoon, cup and mug. The sister reads from a prayerbook, holding a crucifix before the dying woman's eyes. It is impossible to tell, at the very moment of death, whether those eyes are open or shut, dead or alive.

From the placement of these two scenes of the dying it is clear that at St. John's Hospital of Bruges, in the 18th century, patients did not go out with a whimper, but with a

115 Last rites, Beerblock painting

116 Deathbed, Beerblock painting

shout. The dying were of foremost importance there – at the opposite pole from those dying in hospitals nowadays, alone, at the end of a corridor, guiltily avoided by their physicians who cannot cure, and nurses for whom their predicament is a kind of reproach.

The one medical reference in this painting is the physician or apothecary being shown a patient by one of the sisters. With notebook in hand and quill pen between his teeth, he is taking a man's pulse (it is the men's half of the ward).

In the foreground of his painting the artist practically plunges us into the cookpots of this Flemish hospital. The table from which dinner is served is at the kitchen end of the ward; according to the plan, the kitchen is behind the viewer to the right. There is a large pot for meat, which was served with the soup, in a metal plate with curved rim; two smaller pots are perhaps for special diets, between them a

118   Serving dinner, Beerblock painting

117   Taking a pulse, Beerblock painting

saucepan with what looks like eggs. One sister adds a flat crusty bread to each plate, another tastes the food to make sure it is good enough for Christ's poor.

At the far right of our painting an emergency case has just been brought in. The ambulance is a sedan chair with bearers, one of whom adjusts his stocking, the other points toward their burden in a wholly unnecessary gesture.

There is really no mistaking her, her clothes have been hastily stripped off and dropped on the floor, and she has been dressed in the hospital's white gown with red collar. Unconscious, she is being lifted into bed. The nurses are what we today would want nurses to be: all concern and gentleness. The woman in the cubicle behind is very much concerned with what is going on. Tipped over in the next cubicle toward us from the unconscious newcomer is that familiar object, the pottie.

119 Ambulance bearers, Beerblock painting

120 Putting the new patient to bed, Beerblock painting

8 SMALL HOMES FOR THE OLD

If any age ought to understand the principle of small separate dwellings for old people it is ours. People are living much longer and every day we see mansions sold off for far less money than the owner must pay to get two rooms in a Home with a guarantee of lifetime care. It's a gamble, in some cases the rule is that the property reverts to the establishment at death, whether death comes in two days or twenty years. The patient population of the Home is subdivided according to physical mobility and mental alertness, and there is an infirmary for the care of chronics or the lightly indisposed. But in real illness residents are sent to an acute care hospital, the Home has no facilities to treat them.

The two rooms usually bring with them a tiny kitchen for breakfasts, the other two meals being taken in a community dining hall. One must be ambulatory to get to it, therefore being ambulatory is a prerequisite for admission.

Look back as far as you will, when the old could afford it they bought privacy, though on the very tiniest scale. When, in a charity hospital, the old could not afford it, approximate privacy was manoeuvered by subdivision: the late 13th century open ward of the Holy Ghost Hospital, Lübeck, was cubicled in 1820 with two main corridors – one for men, one for women.

123   Holy Ghost Hospital, Lübeck, Germany

121   Almshouses for the old (Hospital der Kindren Alyns, Ghent, Belgium, now a Folklore Museum). These attached houses were added to a 14th century chapel in the early 16th century.

122   The smallest possible room of one's own: Interior of a cubicle at Lübeck

Another instance of cubicling, this time for women only: the once-open hall of the Hospital of the Blessed Mary, Chichester, England, 1290. The roof slopes steeply until the eaves almost reach the ground. The interior side aisles were curtained off by wooden scrollwork partitions in

124   Center aisle, Hospital of the Blessed Mary, Chichester, England, 1290

Restoration times, so that under the eaves could be tucked eight tiny two-room flats, sharing four chimneys – one specifically dated 1680. In 1965, these rooms, lived in today, underwent major improvements, and the kitchens acquired an electric cooker and refrigerator.

125 Behind the screen, Hospital of the Blessed Mary, Chichester, England

The majority of such housing, including some of today's condominiums, harks back to the monastic cloister, specifically to the Carthusian (charterhouse) the first of which was built in that form in 1219. (Today we omit a church, which was an essential part of the original complex.) On this plan was built the Hospital of St. Cross, Winchester, England, still functioning according to its original purpose. It was founded by Bishop Henry du Blois for 13 poor brethren, who still wear black, and it was enlarged in 1444 by Cardinal Beaufort to include 2 priests and 35 brethren, when it was renamed "the almshouse of noble poverty" – i.e. decayed gentlemen, "the embarrassed poor," who wear red. The three sisters who cared for them were confined to the infirmary, site of their labors, and to a passage leading into the upper reaches of the church from which they could listen to the Mass.

One of the old men had died here during the night, and tradition dictated that half the door of the tower entrance be closed until the body was removed from the premises. The far entrance is to the church.

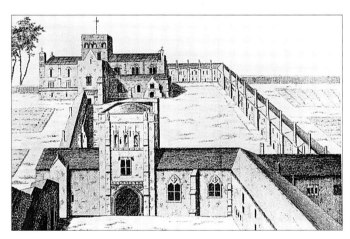

127   Elevation, Hospital of St. Cross, Winchester, England, 1444

126   Main entrance, Hospital of St. Cross, Winchester, England, 1444

113

The pensioners are leaving the church service, where surely they prayed for the soul of their departed brother. Each heads toward his own two-storey dwelling, his own till death. This is the almshouse Trollope wrote about in his novel, *The Warden.* If you ask today at the gatehouse, they will give you the usual wayfarer's dole, bread and ale.

128   Courtyard, Hospital of St. Cross, Winchester, England

A much smaller surviving 15th century almshouse is God's House (Hôtel-Dieu), Ewelme, England (*you-elm*; American soldiers stationed at an airfield nearby during the last war, unable to pronounce it, called it Benson). The charity was founded in 1436 by the Duke of Suffolk, whose wife (Chaucer's granddaughter) is buried in the church of the complex. Down a steep hill from the church (left) is a tiny cloister for pensioners (right), and at the bottom of the hill is a schoolhouse. Sir William Osler was master here while he was Regius Professor of Medicine at Oxford (1904-1919).

The cloister is tiny, the lens of a camera enlarges it.

Thirteen poor folk were to be lodged here, the number thirteen a reference to Christ and the Twelve Apostles. Each unit contains a living room and sink on the ground floor, then, up a flight of stairs so steep one must almost mount them on hands and knees, storage space and a very small bedroom. A bank of toilets had been added – at the end of open corridors. Thus in 1967 only seven of the twelve apartments were occupied, by men and women who seemingly cared more for beauty than convenience. Most poor people look for council housing (what Americans call "a project") in modern flats.

129   God's House, Ewelme, England

130, 131, 132   Inside one unit, God's House, Ewelme

134   Looking across the court, God's House, Ewelme, England

133   A corner of the court, God's House, Ewelme

135   Mrs. Munday in her living room, Ewelme

All around England you can see the two facing rows of small houses with a church at the top of the street, or the two ranges to either side of a small chapel, that denote almshouse, shelter for the old. The Netherlands is another place you see this. Here are half a dozen such dwellings tucked under the cliff of St. Bavo's Church, Haarlem.

Proveniers Hofje, Haarlem, Netherlands, was founded in 1591. *A Hofje* is a Dutch retirement home. It is in the form of a hollow square of attached little houses round an open court.

136 Almshouses, St. Bavo's Church, Haarlem, Netherlands

137 Proveniers Hofje, Haarlem, Netherlands, 1591

The Hospice de Pot, Amersfoort, Netherlands, is a hospice dedicated to feeding people, as the name denotes. Its symbol is a three-legged pot with the Holy Ghost hovering over it in the form of a dove.

The Pot Brethren gave out food to "quiet paupers" (as distinct from vagabonds, who came begging) at an earlier location from 1447. The Pot chapel, still standing, was originally the chapel of a plague hospital, a common pesthouse for the poor all tumbled together plus a few little individual houses for the infected rich. From August 1635 to November 1637, 415 people died in the pesthouse and only 158 recovered. At that point the Pot Brethren added to the first Work of Mercy, Feeding the Hungry, the last Work of Mercy, Burying the Dead – which they did in the churchyard.

After 1667, there was no more plague in Amersfoort. Seventy years later the big pesthouse was demolished, but the little houses were rented out and many more were built round the churchyard, until by the twentieth century it was completely surrounded by two-storey attached row houses, with flowers where tombstones should be.

139   Emblem of the Hospice de Pot, Amersfoort, Netherlands

138   Pensioners' homes and the church, Hospice de Pot, Amersfoort

141   The scale, Hospice de Pot, Amersfoort

140   The oven, Hospice de Pot, Amersfoort   142   Tokens for bread, Hospice de Pot, Amersfoort

Throughout the centuries, bread was given out once a week. The oven baked it, the scales weighed it out. The room in which this was done is now kept as a museum. Each week, when the bread had been baked, the chapel bell tolled and people from the little houses and from the town trooped in to receive rye bread, butter with it always, sometimes even meat. When the cattle were leanest in the spring, hens began to lay again and eggs were distributed.

People qualified to receive alms had collected a token, and as they handed in their bags for food they surrendered it and received another. One week it was a copper token and the next week bronze, so no one could claim the dole twice in a single week. Downstairs from the bakery was the room where bread and butter were given out every Thursday, at the ringing of the bell. The poor received money as well, but for that they had to go to church. Protestant pastors would visit the poor every week and give them a different token. When the collection was taken in church, they put their token in, and this was the sign they had been to church. Then they got their money.

For more than 500 years – from 1447 to 1974 – the custom of bread distribution at the Hospice de Pot continued unbroken. By that time social assistance made it redundant. For the last time, on Christmas 1974, they rang the bell, and gave out loaves in the church.

People were sorry to see the old way go. It had been such a pleasant get-together.

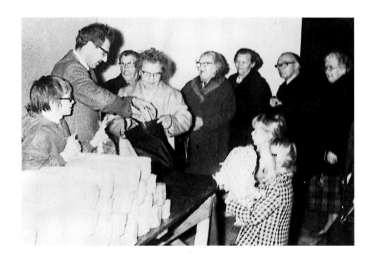

143   The last dole, Hospice de Pot, Amersfoort, Netherlands

9 MEDICINE AND PHARMACY

As we have seen, the hospital of all centuries up to and through the 18th offered shelter, food, nursing care, and above all religious attention. A medical presence was noticeably minimal. Medicine itself was of limited effect in those days. For a thousand years, medicos had been dominated by the authority of Galen (a Greek, second century A.D.) and, forgetting Galen's own injunction to observe and experiment, memorized and could reel off by heart his experimental results. Galen had had almost no access to human bodies to dissect. His experimental observations were based on the bodies of animals, whatever he could lay his hands on, including the large apes. Being dead set on affirming a divine plan underlying his data, he concocted the connecting bits and pronounced his conclusions applicable to man. So during the Renaissance the Galenic text was read from the professorial chair by a scholar who never lifted his eyes to see if what his authority said was true. The body before him on the stone table was dissected by an assistant.

We can imagine the lesson taking place in this, the smallest anatomy theatre in Europe, a 16th century artistic treasure which still stands three feet from the rear door of a ward of the Ospedale del Ceppo ("*ceppo*" means poor box) in Pistoia, Italy. There was room for only twelve students on the curving benches (on which some of them carved their names).

To eliminate illness, the chief recourse was a process of elimination: bleeding and purging these physicians laid waste their hours – and very often their patients as well. In one of the seven great works by the Master of Alkmaar, 1504 (which, being seven in number, you might know would deal with the Seven Works of Mercy), "Visiting the Sick" shows how the treatment operated in a hospital of the time

144   Anatomical theatre, Hospital del Ceppo, Pistoia, Italy, 16th century

145   "Visiting the Sick", The Seven Works of Mercy, the Master of Alkmaar, Rijksmuseum, Amsterdam, 1504

and how the victims – beg pardon, patients, felt about it. The figure of the Christ appears in each of the seven views; his presence, here certainly, a therapeutic necessity.

The physician at the first bed is taking a pulse, making stern eye-contact with the patient. The nurse arrives with the potion.

In the background is the before and the after. The patient to the left is being ordered to take an emetic. That

146 Physician and patient, "Visiting the Sick", The Master of Alkmaar
      (detail)

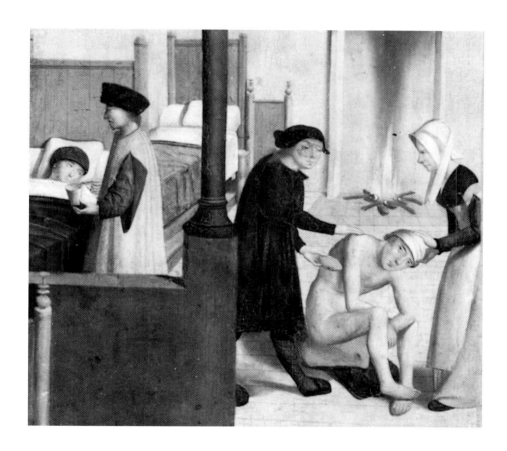

stern pointing finger! He gazes over wistfully at its outcome (literally). For the patient on the stool? pot? stone? is in some anguish as you can tell from his feet. The nurse holds his head. In some pictures that show actual spewing, the nurse always holds the head. Here an assistant, with comforting gesture, offers a bowl that seems undersized for the consequences.

As always the patient is naked, save for a turban, but there's a good roaring fire.

147   Physic and its consequences, The Master of Alkmaar (detail), 1504

Drugs were respected, for they cost money. They were kept in their own cabinet, the more valuable in a section of smaller drawers with its own doors that locked, as shown here in the restored pharmacy of the Hospital de S. Juan Bautista, Toledo, Spain (1562). The pharmacy is now a museum, the hospital is used as a school and for civic events.

This is known as the "eye" of the drug cabinet.

149   Restored pharmacy, Hospital de S. Juan Bautista, Toledo, Spain, 1562

148   Section for precious drugs, Pharmacy, Hospital de S. Juan Bautista, Toledo

Now let us consider surgery in the hospital. This painting, as crude as the surgical methods it illustrates, shows what must have been an outpatient surgical clinic held in an inpatient ward at St. Catherine's Hospital, Utrecht, in the 17th century. (It is also possible the artist was trying to record in one painting, of which we show details, two departments of this hospital.)

The inpatients here are actually clothed in more than the turbans on their heads, and they lie two by two. It is clear that only bandages in the hand were to be used, those dropped on the floor being very much dirtier (or, perhaps, the black squares of flooring were painted first, and the colour seeped through).

Vesalius, in the 16th century, did his own dissections and rewarded his medical contemporaries and heirs with a splendid series of woodcuts (executed by an excellent Renaissance artist) showing the true anatomy of the human body; he also encouraged doctors to think, as he tried to think, according to the evidence of their own senses. Ambroise Paré, in the 16th century, not only taught himself to be a surgeon of unprecedented skill, but discredited cautery in favor of soothing oils for healing amputations. In the 17th century, William Harvey solved the puzzle of the circulation of the blood. These findings were accepted, disseminated, even seized upon, yet medical practice itself was very slow to change.

150   St. Catherine's Hospital, Utrecht, Netherlands, 17th century

151   St. Catherine's Hospital, Utrecht, Netherlands, 17th century

There is a print dated 1746, labeled "The Pest House in Munich." Nonsense! It is a compendium of human ailments and healing interventions, half of which are religious and straight out of the Work of Mercy we have known as "Visiting the Sick." Aside from the three figures in the margins, all of whom have to do with the bestowing of alms, the first duo in the lower left-hand corner of the picture itself illustrate "giving drink to the thirsty," and the background is occupied with no less than four figures "giving food to the hungry," behind whom two others are bearing out a body in

a sheet, for "burying the dead." Behind the "thirsty" pair is a scene of the administration of Last Rites to a dying patient in bed.

But the other episodes have a more or less medical context and add up to the medical and surgical interventions practicable in the mid-18th century. From left to right, foreground: a cripple with hand-crutches. The operation of couching for cataract, no operating table, no bed, no chair even (whether the figure is half kneeling for the convenience of the surgeon or of the artist is hard to say).

152   *Not* "The Pest House in Munich" but all 18th century medicine in
      one hospital room, 1746

Amputation of a leg, and this patient is at least stretched out – recumbent is hardly the word. Next, lower right corner, a patient bedridden with dropsical legs; and behind her a man whose belly is distended, and a woman at whose naked breast a medical assistant dabs with an expression of alarm. A peck of medicine to a ton of misery. There are specific hospital notes in the background: a bent old woman representing all those aged that the hospital sheltered until they died; inpatients left and right background, two to a bed; and between them cells for the insane along the back wall. Through small windows in the locked cell doors insane heads can be seen howling. Allegory? Alas!

In a frontispiece of 1783 the physician is seen as hero, though the arms he bears are brittle. He stands defiant, hand on sword, center foreground right, trying to stare down the Adversary, a skeleton with scythe who breaks through the central door on the left wall. There are medical reinforcements: a second physician ready to enter at the opposite door, and a dark enigmatic figure foreground center, who may be holding a bleeding bowl in one hand and flask of urine in the other, which he studies.

The astounding aspect of this picture is its total lack, in a hospital ward, of religious reference, there being in the rear wall a mere central door and two windows.

The same underemphasis on a religious note is stated architecturally at the Krankenspital of Bamberg, Germany, 1788. In a totally symmetrical building, à la 18th century, who would guess that the four windows under the oval oculus in the central pediment are the main windows of a central chapel? A minimal steeple overhead is the sole clue. And yet, within, there is a rather more other-worldly accommodation: windows in the side walls of the chapel carry the Mass acoustically, if not visually, into the men's wards to one side and women's to the other. Open doors placed enfilade (one right behind the other) next to the outer wall convey the words splendidly from ward to ward – and privy to privy, for in this hospital the narrow walls of both ward and privy have windows through the wall of the front facade, and ten-bed wards are interspersed with narrow four- or eight-seat privy corridors. So the Mass may pass to the far end of the building (C-shaped; beds in the two arms are out of hearing) to the edification of many, a distinctly this-worldly touch.

153   The physician takes on a battle with Death, 1783

154   Central section of the façade, Krankenspital, Bamberg, Germany, 1788

The rear court at Bamberg has a very German look. But then, so do the hospitals of other countries look like the rest of that country's architecture. Whatever purpose-built amenities they may incorporate, and until the end of the 18th century these were very few, the general effect is of a basic building plan to which patients have to adapt themselves as best they can. When it came to the customary division of the sexes in a hospital, the symmetry of 18th century building forms answered very well.

> *It's a very strange thing*
> *Just as strange as can be*
> *That whatever Miss T eats*
> *Turns into Miss T–*

And in this context we can interpret Walter de la Mare's poem to mean that whatever Copenhagen builds turns into Copenhagen architecture: in this case, the 18th century Naval Hospital.

When you cross a border between one European country and another, everything changes, from what is considered inevitable for breakfast, to the accepted standards of polite social behavior. So from country to country the hospitals, of whatever age, take on the characteristics of general buildings in that country at that age.

156   Naval Hospital, Copenhagen, Denmark, 18th century

155   Rear court, Krankenspital, Bamberg, Germany

Belgian architecture of the 17th century is typified in this door to the Infirmary of the Byloke Hospital, Ghent – behind which can be found the room where the feet of the poor were washed on Maundy Thursday.

St. Elizabeths-gasthuis, Haarlem, Netherlands, completed 1588, is now the Franz Hals Museum. This is anything but purpose-built architecture.

Our Lady's Hospital (Onze Lieve Vrouwe-hospital) of Cortrai, Belgium, was founded in the 13th century for women in childbed and for foundlings. Its buildings date mainly from the 17th century and are still in use.

158 Onze Lieve Vrouwe-hospitaal, Cortrai, Belgium, 17th century

157 Infirmary, Byloke Hospital, Ghent, Belgium, 17th century

159 St. Elizabeths-gasthuis, Haarlem, Netherlands, 1588

137

In 17th and 18th century France a real effort was made to
help the patient by building the risers of stairs deliberately
low.

160   Steps to the chapel, Hôpital St. Jacques, Besançon, France, founded
      1667

161   Main staircase, Hôpital St. Sepulchre, Salins-les-Bains, France, 1687

This is the dining room window of the Potterie Hospital,
Bruges, Belgium, in 1965 when its courtyard still existed.
The view can no longer be seen.

162   Dining room window, Potterie Hospital, Bruges, Belgium

The 18th century hospital of Langres, Burgundy, France, had two slanting (and matching) wings attached to a central church two stories high, which had entrances from the two stories of wards both at its ground floor level and to its balcony. The side wings were also symmetrical, with a central door. These photographs were taken just in time. The hospital was being used in 1971 as an old age home, with a few mental defectives mixed in. A decade or so later the building was found abandoned, grass was growing between the stones of the front steps.

163 Hôpital, Langres, France, 18th century

These are patients of the hospital at Langres.

His mind's all there!

164   Patients, Hôpital, Langres

165   Blind patient, Hôpital, Langres

166   Male Patient, Hôpital, Langres

For once, the photographer arrived in the nick of time. The pharmacy of the Hospital of S. Juan de Dios (Hospital Provincial) of Jaen, Spain, had been in constant operation for two hundred years. In two weeks the pharmacy was scheduled to be modernized. The old trappings were to be moved out to a museum. Between them, the pharmacist and his father had worked in this pharmacy 100 years.

(Compare this lamp with the one in Figure 11, "The Fourth Work of Mercy..." This one has the other beat all hollow.)

167   Overhead lamp, Pharmacy, Hospital de San Juan de Dios, Jaen, Spain

The 18th century pharmacy of Hôpital St. Sepulchre, Salins
les Bains, Burgundy, France, was treated here and there as a
museum, but since it was still in use, a compromise had to
be reached between antique jars and antibiotics. Above
arm's reach, the jars were allowed to prevail.

168   Pharmacy, Hôpital St. Sepulchre, Salins les Bains, France

10 OPPOSITE ENDS OF THE SPECTRUM

The range of institutions in simultaneous operation under the rubric "hospital" at the end of the 18th century may be suggested by contrasting two utterly dissimilar institutions: the medieval St. Nikolaus-Spital of Cues, Germany (1451) and the newly expanded and modernized (1784) Allgemeines Krankenhaus of Vienna.

The first was tiny, the second vast. This meant the same as it might today: personal attention versus standardized treatment, hand-wrought building details versus mass production.

169 Allgemeines Krankenhaus,
     Vienna, Austria, 1784

The first was privately endowed by Cardinal Nikolaus Cusanus, the second was a state institution, abundantly subsidized by Emperor Joseph II, who was the state, and whose favorite charity it was.

The first was an old age home for pensioners. The second was a general hospital for the full range of acute illnesses.

The first was still completely of its time: old school. The second anticipated new beginnings. For a change was coming over the hospital after a thousand years, the very concept was being reconsidered, but at the Allgemeines Krankenhaus only a little, so far; and at Cues, not ever.

170   St. Nikolaus-Spital, Cues, Germany, 1451

148

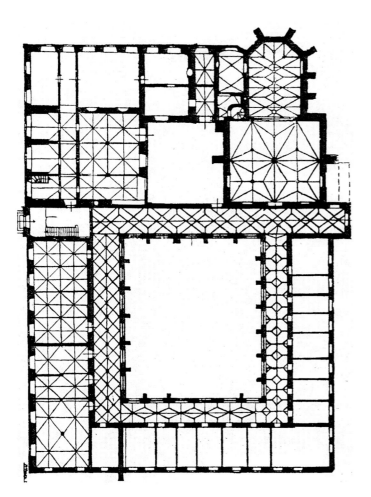

St. Nikolaus-Spital, Cues, is built on a courtyard plan dis-tantly reminiscent of Spanish hospitals; the apsed chapel however does not lie parallel to the court and open upon the street, but at right angles to the court, opening on the arcade. Beyond the chapel on the eastern wing is a feature unique in hospitals: the Cardinal's elegant private library. On the upper floor of the northern wing are two open wards for 21 pauper patients, later cubicled (indicated by the cross-hatching). Around the southern and western sides of the courtyard are private rooms for retired ("decayed") noble-men and priests, yet one more instance of the principle of privacy for the upper classes.

This version at Cues of "Visiting the Sick" is indicative of wealthy sponsors.

171 Plan of St. Nikolaus-Spital, Cues, Germany

172 Visiting the Sick, St. Nikolaus-Spital, Cues, Germany

All the windows but two have different designs. One window shows the sun and the moon. The courtyard is glassed in. We are far north of Andalusia.

173   Detail, one window, St. Nikolaus-Spital, Cues, Germany
174   Windows around the arcade, St. Nikolaus-Spital, Cues, Germany
175   Courtyard arcade, St. Nikolaus-Spital, Cues, Germany

The pendants of seven ceiling ribs from the South to the Chapel door, that opens on the arcade, read like a German version of Chaucer – a contemporary of Nikolaus Cusanus.

The clock over the stairs at the entrance was appropriate for the old men who lived here in 1967 – if not exactly cheery.

176   Faces on the pendants, Chapel Door, St. Nikolaus-Spital, Cues

177   The clock over the stair, St. Nikolaus-Spital, Cues

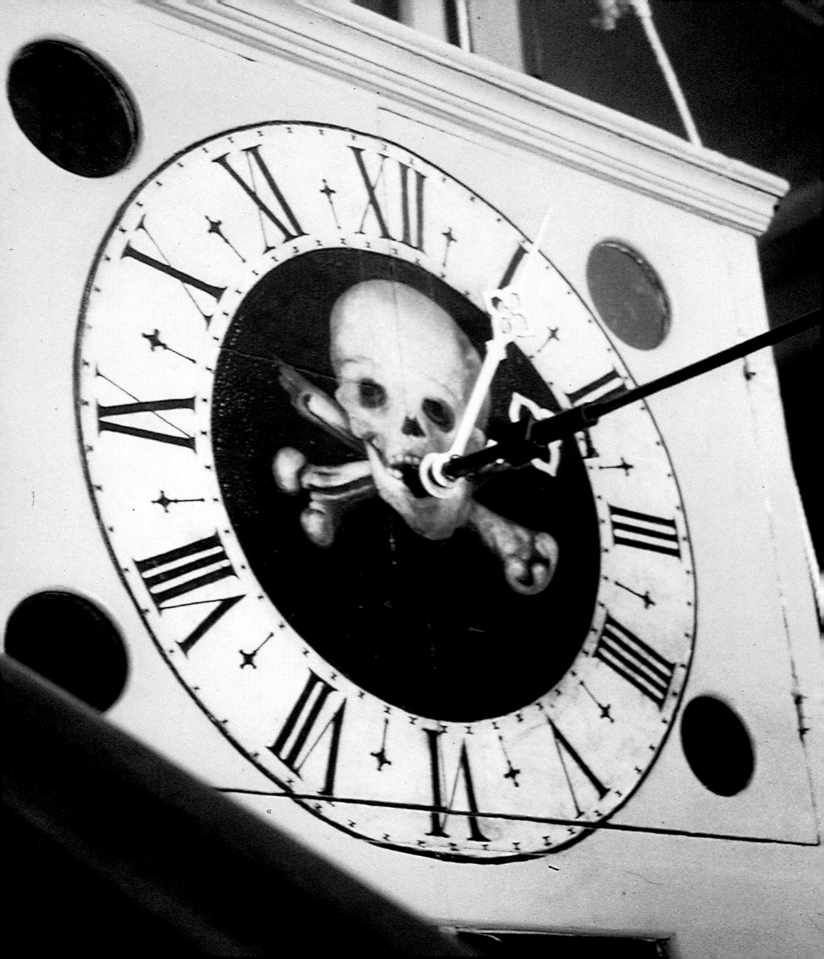

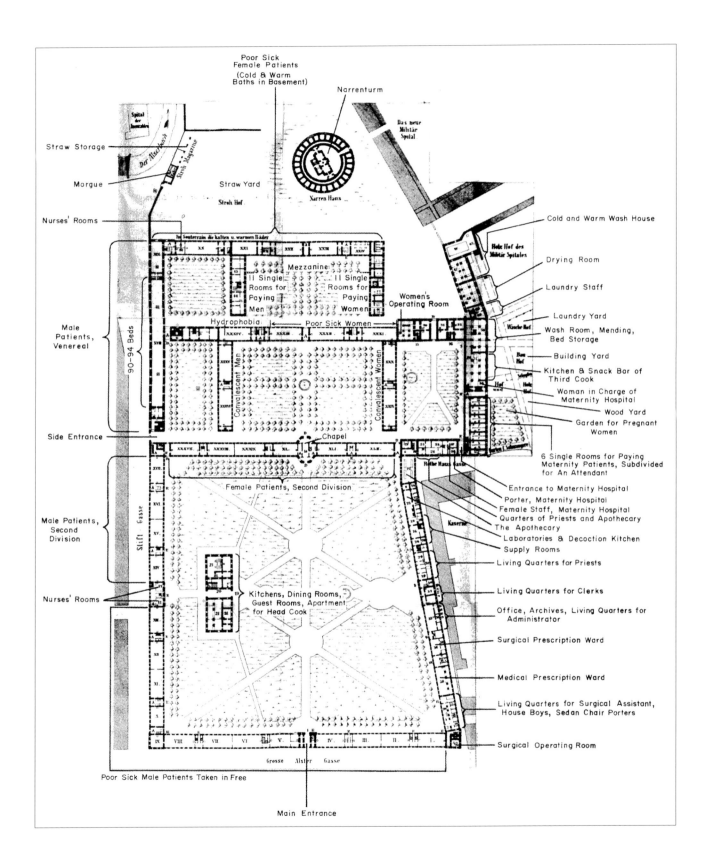

Poor Sick
Female Patients
(Cold & Warm
Baths in Basement)

Narrenturm

Das neue
Militär
Spital

Straw Storage

Spital
der
Invaliden

Der Hachuch

Morgue

Stroh Magazine

Straw Yard

Nurses' Rooms

Stroh Hof

Narren Haus

Cold and Warm Wash House

Holz Hof des
Militär Spitales

Drying Room

Im Souterrain die kalten u. warmen Bäder

Mezzanine:

Laundry Staff

XX   XXI

XXII   XXIII

XXIV

Laundry Yard

II Single
Rooms for
Paying
Men

II Single
Rooms for
Paying
Women

Women's
Operating Room

Wäsche Hof

Wash Room, Mending,
Bed Storage

Male
Patients,
Venereal

90–94 Beds

Hydrophobia

Poor Sick Women

Building Yard

XXXIV

XXXIII   XXXII

XXXI

Bau
Hof

Kitchen & Snack Bar of
Third Cook

Convalescent Men

Convalescent Women

Schlacht
Hof

Woman in Charge of
Maternity Hospital

Wood Yard

Garden for Pregnant
Women

Side Entrance

Chapel

XXXVII   XXXVIII   XXXIX   XL.

XLI   XLII

Rothe Haus Gasse

6 Single Rooms for Paying
Maternity Patients, Subdivided
for An Attendant

Female Patients, Second Division

Entrance to Maternity Hospital
Porter, Maternity Hospital
Female Staff, Maternity Hospital
Quarters of Priests and Apothecary
The Apothecary
Laboratories & Decoction Kitchen
Supply Rooms

Male Patients,
Second
Division

Stift Gasse

Kaserne

Living Quarters for Priests

Living Quarters for Clerks

Nurses' Rooms

Kitchens, Dining Rooms,
Guest Rooms, Apartment
for Head Cook

Office, Archives, Living Quarters for
Administrator

Surgical Prescription Ward

Medical Prescription Ward

Living Quarters for Surgical Assistant,
House Boys, Sedan Chair Porters

IX   VIII   VII   VI   V.   IV   III.   II.   I.

Surgical Operating Room

Grosse Alster Gasse

Poor Sick Male Patients Taken in Free

Main Entrance

154

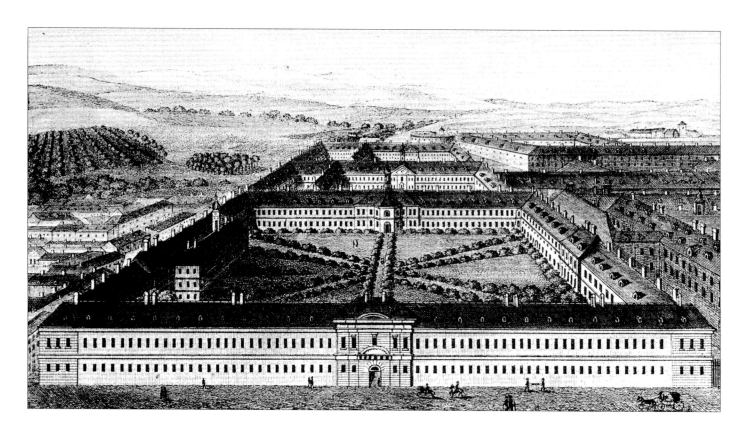

Perhaps the contrast illustrated here for the 18th century could be duplicated today if we set side by side an established bustling metropolitan medical center and one of the more modest of our new hospices for the dying. In that case the new form would be the tiny caretaking place, with its concern for the individual, and the old form the vast medical complex with its inflexible emphasis on cure. At the Allgemeines Krankenhaus or General Hospital of Vienna, the wave of the future was headed precisely opposite. The revenues of many small endowed foundations were confiscated to raise the funds for this centralized, rationally-organized state hospital. The poor supported by those diverse shelters were separated from the ill and sent into the country, where they could be more cheaply maintained. The sick were assembled in a 2,000 bed acute care hospital, a huge complex of seven courts parts of which had been used since 1693 as a poorhouse, veterans' home, even as

housing for penniless students. At great expense it was updated and, with so much horizontal space to dispose of, categories of illness were kept separate and assigned to specific areas. How much hospital history is captured in the mere labels on the first- and second-floor plans of the Allgemeines Krankenhaus!

The normal ward was a manageable 18-22 beds, but wards for syphilitics could have as many as 94 beds. Stairs, vestibules, kitchens, privies between wards are marked A on the ground floor plan, B on the second floor plan. The façade reproduced as a contrast to the entire building at Cues is *just the bottom row* of buildings along Grosse Alster Gasse.

Although there is a chapel at the center rear of the first great square, in its traditional placement opposite the main entrance, we sense that religious influence has been significantly attenuated.

179   Allgemeines Krankenhaus, Vienna, about 1834

178   Allgemeines Krankenhaus, Vienna: first floor plan

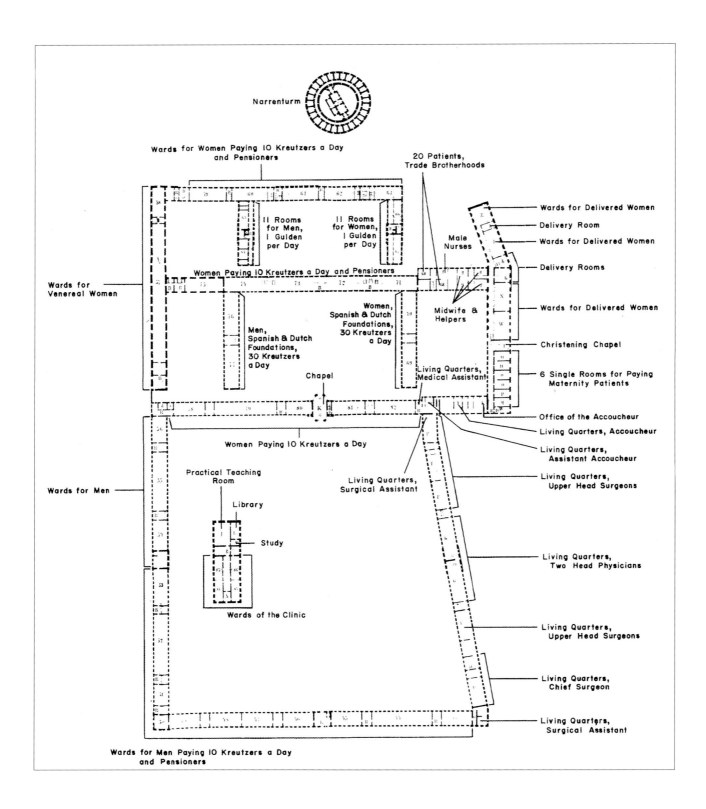

Narrenturm

Wards for Women Paying 10 Kreutzers a Day
and Pensioners

20 Patients,
Trade Brotherhoods

11 Rooms
for Men,
1 Gulden
per Day

11 Rooms
for Women,
1 Gulden
per Day

Male
Nurses

Women Paying 10 Kreutzers a Day and Pensioners

Wards for
Venereal Women

Wards for Delivered Women

Delivery Room

Wards for Delivered Women

Delivery Rooms

Women,
Spanish & Dutch
Foundations,
30 Kreutzers
a Day

Midwife &
Helpers

Wards for Delivered Women

Men,
Spanish & Dutch
Foundations,
30 Kreutzers
a Day

Christening Chapel

Chapel

Living Quarters,
Medical Assistant

6 Single Rooms for Paying
Maternity Patients

Office of the Accoucheur

Living Quarters, Accoucheur

Women Paying 10 Kreutzers a Day

Living Quarters,
Assistant Accoucheur

Practical Teaching
Room

Living Quarters,
Surgical Assistant

Living Quarters,
Upper Head Surgeons

Library

Wards for Men

Study

Living Quarters,
Two Head Physicians

Wards of the Clinic

Living Quarters,
Upper Head Surgeons

Living Quarters,
Chief Surgeon

Living Quarters,
Surgical Assistant

Wards for Men Paying 10 Kreutzers a Day
and Pensioners

156

A religious presence in the ward was slight. True, this was a ward of the eye clinic, where patients with cataract operations were really not expected to die.

At the same time there was from the outset a new impetus toward solvency, a concern about money. It can be read on the very plan: "Wards for women paying 10 kreutzers a day," etc. This hospital charged on a sliding scale, an innovation shocking to contemporaries accustomed to charitable Christian institutions for the destitute and the Seven Works of Mercy. What you paid determined grade of food and service. There were four grades, the lowest for true paupers, who paid nothing, and got the worst of both.

Christian charity was proving unequal to its task. Partly this was the curse of bigness. From the 17th century on the disadvantaged were gathered in larger and larger groups in ever more immense institutions, centralized under the state in 1656, in Paris where the charitable hospitals were confiscated and became what was called the Hôpital Général, with the direct backing of the king. It was very bad for patients, but very much in harmony with the spirit of the times – centralize! rationalize! – and so the concept spread from country to country, until each state, proud of its power and modernity, had introduced its own General Hospital. The falling off of charity can also be partially attributed to human frailty and a loosening of belief in spiritual redemption through alms.

One instance of the shift explains much: the rise and fall of the baciners of the Hospital de la Santa Creu in Barcelona. A *bacinero* is one who passes the plate for the poor box. Messengers gathering charity went from town to town on the hospital's business and enjoyed remarkable privileges: they were under the king's protection, they were permitted to use "forbidden weapons" and to display the royal arms, they were exempt from toll, from being taken prisoner, and from being impounded to take any job in any city, town, or place where they were baciners. They could travel freely to beg alms for the hospitals and were not to be treated as vagabonds. They were welcomed in a way that must have done their hearts good – all the bells were set to chiming, and during the charity drive no wedding, baptism, or burial could take place.

But the alms-gatherers did not always bring a proper attitude to the job. One after the other absconded with the funds. Christian charity works well enough, but only when all agree to it. By the middle of the 18th century, the administration of the Hospital de la Santa Creu of Barcelona decided to farm out the collection on a one-time basis, for a fee. This was a mistake. People no longer felt they were giving directly to the hospital, nor did they feel called upon to contribute to drives set up in a way that would benefit the collectors. By the middle of the 19th century the baciners had disappeared. This led inevitably to state-supported hospitals.

William James once remarked, "The whole modern scientific organization of charity is a consequence of the failure of simply giving alms."

Joseph II, Emperor of Austria, under whose direct guidance the Allgemeines Krankenhaus took the form it did, had his own ways of raising money for it. Erna Lesky tells us about them:

"When a Bavarian count. . . felt the absolute necessity of becoming a prince, and had admittedly provided no services to the state, the 250,000 gulden that he offered Joseph for this elevation was too little. The emperor made the count pay 500,000 gulden and used these for his favorite creation."

181   The vestiges of religion, Allgemeines Krankenhaus, Vienna

180   Allgemeines Krankehaus, Vienna: second floor plan

The building of the vast complex that is closest to its original, unaltered state is the Eye Clinic.

Windows were kept high so that cross ventilation might be accomplished well above the patients' heads, and could be adjusted at three different levels.

An entry from the street to the court was in three parts as well: a regular door for pedestrians, two flaps for ordinary carts or carriages, and a top piece for loftier equipages, all separately operable.

183   Window construction, Allgemeines Krankenhaus, Vienna

182   Eye Clinic, Allgemeines Krankenhaus, Vienna

184   Entrance arrangement, Allgemeines Krankenhaus, Vienna

Three divisions of the Allgemeines Krankenhaus were built from scratch under Joseph II: the round tower at the rear of the site – the Narrenturm for the insane; the maternity court; and the orphanage. For the maternity division the key word was confidentiality. Women illegally pregnant could approach it by a locked and guarded private alleyway, "wearing masks, veiled, or made unrecognizable in any manner that they wished." They could stay half a year if they wanted to, working for their keep if they were poor, or if they were rich, in possession of a two-room private apartment, the second room being for their maid. The women's names were never recorded, save in a sealed envelope handed in at admission which was to be opened only in the event of their death. They could keep the baby or consign it to the hospital.

Maternity division and orphanage were interdependent. You could not undertake to deliver a pregnant woman without devising some arrangement for the child when born. These were precautions against child murder; a child was regarded as the wealth of the nation, a future worker for the state. (The 18th century did not suffer from overpopulation.) Legend has it that Santo Spirito Hospital of Rome was founded in the 15th century because Pope Innocent III had dreamed that fishermen were bringing him strange fish caught in their nets, the corpses of newborn babies from the Tiber.

The problem was universal. The cause: human frailty; the result: an unwanted child; the outcome: a corpse in the Tiber or whatever water lay handy. The salvaged babies urgently needed wet nurses. Since there are no available representations of these necessary arrangements at the Allgemeines Krankenhaus, we can see wet nurses at work in a fresco at Santo Spirito Hospital, Rome, in an earlier day.

For centuries abandoned babies were admitted to hospitals via the ruota, a baby-sized receptacle operating vertically on the principle of a revolving door, or horizontally like a mail-box, behind which waited a representative of the maternity service (very often a religious order). The mother (or whoever) might deposit the baby, tug the bell, and run. Here it is seen in operation in Paris, where the contraption was known as "*le tour*." (Of a male infant abandoned at the main gate of Old Blockley, the Philadelphia, Pennsylvania, Almshouse, in the late 18th century, in a basket tied to the latch, it was suggested in the *Book of Daily Occurrences*: "His surname is either George Gate, Benjamin Basket or Lawrence Latch, at your service.")

185   "*Le tour d'abandon*" Paris, 19th century

186   Wet nurses at work, Santo Spirito Hospital, Rome, 16th century

PART THREE

OUT OF THE DARKNESS

191   Fire at the Hôtel-Dieu, Paris, 1772

Les Religieuses de l'hotel Dieu de Paris estante a la Riuiere.
A. Laueure des Cinq Cents Draps, qui ce fait vne fois le mois, ou touttes
les meres et nonices si doiuent trouuer.
B. les petites lauendieres, lauant les Draps, trois fois le jour, Scauoir.
de puis quatre heures du matin jusqu'à neuf heures, de puis
midy, jusqu'à deux heures, et de puis quatre heures,
jusqu'à sept heures du soir. Guerard ex

11 THE HOTEL-DIEU OF PARIS

Good Lord, what human slaughter! Never have wards, pestilence, famine, rage, blood and all the punishments of heaven together produced anything similar. And nowhere is it as terrible as in Paris at the Hôtel-Dieu... In the House of God in Paris! Is it not a travesty, a true blasphemy to give this name to a house which resembles a bottomless pit, which daily swallows up humanity?

Daignau, *Two Hundred Years of the Charité Hospital in Berlin*

Must charitie be blamed because she has a latitude of hearte? – to suffer all, to solace all, to do good to all? Must they be blamed for choosing rather to save the lives of two in one bedd, than to suffer one of them to die on a dunghill or in a ditch?

An English visitor to Paris, 1666

QUESTIONNAIRE
Sent to contemporary hospitals by the Royal Commission on Hospitals (c. 1785), with answers given by the hospital of Bordeaux (*"UN QUESTIONNAIRE...avec la réponse donnée par l'Hôpital de Bordeaux, papiers de Tenon,"* Quoted in M. Foucault *et al., Les machines a guérir*, 1976, pp. 158-167, *passim.*)

Q. *Is the hospital on a river?*
A. It is situated on a stream called the Devese, that has no water most of the year, and sends out an intolerable stench throughout the hospital.
Q. *What is the usual number of patients?*
A. The usual number of patients is 400, but we could never have had more than 600.

Q. *What is the number of ecclesiastics, officers (men and women), people in all types of service?*
A. Four almoners, 4 physicians, 1 surgeon, and 3 students, 26 female religious, 10 male nurses and 7 female nurses.
Q. *What is the number of wards, and the particular use of each?*
A. Three male fever wards, 2 male surgical wards... 2 wards for fever (women), one for women (surgical).
Q. *Do you wash the floors of the principal wards?*
A. Wooden floors, all of them are washed.
Q. (About the windows, ventilation, number of stories, arrangements for convalescents.)
A. There is cross-ventilation from two sides in certain wards, but all badly aired. Three wards on the ground floor and two below the level of the street. There is only one storey. There is nothing for convalescents, contagious diseases are mingled with the others.
Q. (Detailed questions about beds, how many rows, passages between rows, number of patients in beds, what the beds are made of.)
A. The beds are four feet wide and the sick are kept in them at least two to a bed. The passages between are very tight, the width of the principal passageway proportionate to the size of the ward and they for the most part are all narrow. All the beds are wood and in winter all have serge curtains. Sheets, chemises, pillowcases – no fixed number; despite that as few as possible are given out.
Q. (Detailed question about toilets).
A. No toilets at all in the wards. In each ward a fireplace where frequently the fire is not lit... The patients have close-stools, one to each four patients, emptied once or twice a day in the Devese, whether there is water in it or not. And when a flood of water comes, the ordure is carried into the river.

187 Washing sheets, Hôtel-Dieu of Paris

Q. *Information on the distribution of water, is there enough above all for daily needs, and in case of fire?*

A. No water at all in the house, but a fountain which does not always run, and when water fails, a well is used which furnishes nearly all the water necessary.

Q. *What precautions against fires?*

A. No precaution against fire, but to fall back on prudence.

Q. (Number of all kinds of baths).

A. Nothing of the sort.

Q. *What is the number of sick in an ordinary year, of discharges, of deaths?*

A. One does not wish to know.

Q. *What are the dominant maladies, those easily cured, those resisting cure, those not curable at all?*

A. The dominant maladies are putrid fevers (i.e., typhus).

Q. (Division of patients according to diagnosis.)

A. All the sick are mingled and it often happens that the patients catch scabies from their companions. No pregnant women at all. No treatment at all for the mad, patients with scurvy are mingled with the others as well as the consumptives.

Q. *How much does each patient cost you?*

A. We are unable to know how much each patient costs each day.

Q. *Are patients received with open doors, and without recommendation? Are there patients not accepted at all: what are the diseases not admitted at all?*

A. Every patient is received if, when he presents himself at the door, he is found to have fever. Venereal diseases are excluded from the hospital and are the only diseases not received.

Q. *What care is taken with the clothes of the patients? Do you distinguish between those with vermin and those without, and the clothes of patients entering with contagious diseases?*

A. All the clothes are thrown together, and no effort is made at disinfection.

Q. *Do you give indigents any money to return to their country and subsist for at least a day before returning to work?*

A. We give to those who leave us alive some biscuits which reduces by that much the little money they may have. We give nothing to those who have nothing.

Q. (The morgue: its construction; do you pay attention not to bury the living?)

A. Sometimes we must bring back to the hospital patients already sewn into the sacking who got mixed up with the dead. That room is small and humid.

Q. (What is the portion of food, the half-portion, the quarter portion?)

A. The weight of a quarter portion is four ounces of bread, and besides one gives them a little soup.

Q. *Have you paid any attention to promenades?*

A. There isn't a single place to promenade.

The Royal Infirmary of Edinburgh, a modest, self-contained, C-shaped building with 200 beds, was opened in 1738, and its plans were published with the following superscription: "This Hospital will be open to all the Cureable distressed from what ever Corner of the world they come without restriction." The Hôtel-Dieu of Paris said the same thing – and for a thousand years or so acted upon it. That was the trouble. It is all very well to behave like a medieval hospital while one is a medieval hospital – the Hôtel-Dieu dates back: in tradition to 650 A.D.; in documents to 829; in its first enduring buildings to 1165. It began as a medieval catch-all, but as Paris grew the Hôtel-Dieu could not catch everything. However, it tried, and as a result was drastically overcrowded throughout its history. Diderot put it succinctly in 1765: "The Hôtel-Dieu is the most extensive, populated, rich, and frightful of our hospitals."

There were better and worse centuries. The worst was the 18th, when matters came to a head. In 1777, the English philanthropist John Howard wrote,

"L'Hôpital de St. Louis for the sick, and L'Hôtel de Dieu, are indeed the two worst hospitals that I ever visited. They were so crowded, that I have frequently seen four or five in one bed, some of them dying. In one of my visits at l'Hôtel de Dieu, I observed the number of patients written up to be three thousand six hundred and fifty-five. Over one of the gates of this hospital is the following inscription, which, from its application to such a place, has an air of ridicule and even of profaneness. 'C'est icy la Maison de Dieu, et la Porte du Ciel'" – "This is the House of God, and the door to heaven:"

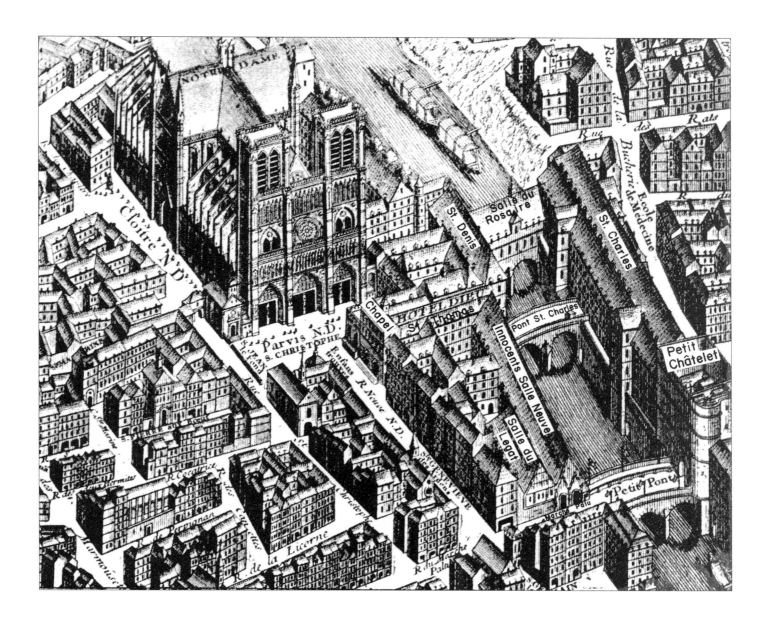

Appropriate enough motto for a hospital whose death rate was twice that of other hospitals; throughout the 18th century, one in four.

The administrative Sisters tried to cover up the state of their hospital with words, which perhaps they even believed; they spoke of "the glory to be the hospital of the kingdom, of Europe, and one might say, of all humanity."

But that was the trouble.

The Hôtel-Dieu of Paris was worse than the hospital in Bordeaux, whose answers to an 18th century questionnaire are certainly not encouraging, though probably average – low average – for the time. At least the Hôtel-Dieu had no real water problem – the Seine ran all the time.

This was the single advantage of a site constricted between Notre Dame Cathedral and the river, with no room to expand. The space had been ample enough for the first

188   A comprehensive view of the Hôtel-Dieu, from the Turgot plan of Paris, 1759

cathedral and the hospital attendant upon it. It was enough even for the basilica hospital attached to the third cathedral (still very early – 1160). But on a 1759 plan of Paris one sees what happened over the centuries on that small triangle of land in front of Notre Dame, between the Salle St. Denis and the Petit Pont. There are four small open courts, amid a pack of buildings in which smelly and noxious events were constantly happening. The Salle du Legat (far larger than and roughly contemporaneous with the hospital in Tonnerre, and of similar form) shared one long wall with the Salle Neuve, while its other long wall opened upon a mere slit of an alleyway. When a bequest was received, a ward was inserted, on some ground still vacant, with no concern for existing structures and no thought whatever of long-range planning. The two immense wards along the Seine happened by luck to face south, and at least received unobstructed breezes from the river, on which nobody could build. But build they did! – the Salle du Rosaire, on a bridge over the river. So, quite aside from the crowding and extraordinary mix of patients in the 17th and 18th centuries, for the *buildings* themselves there was no room. There were no connecting corridors. All communication routes from one building to another led through some ward on its long axis, between two or four rows of beds.

Already, in the 15th century, the Salle Neuve had 85 beds, and each could hold three patients *tête-bêche* (*bêche* is a spade: the middle patient's head lay between the feet of the patients on either side).

189   Laundry shed, Hôtel-Dieu of Paris

When the Salle de Rosaire was built in 1626, madmen were put in a second floor ward communicating directly with one for 300 surgical patients: the howls of the mad took up where the screams of those operated upon left off. On its third floor the ward for madwomen was simply a continuation of a ward for women with fevers; maternity patients were moved in here as well.

One might hope that when the St. Charles building went up across the river, between 1651 and 1661, it would take some of the pressure off this mixed cauldron of human ills, but the new building was, in effect, one open ward. The plan shows enormous wards exchanging their air, and a central staircase to make sure all air would be liberally mixed with that of, say, the smallpox wards on the fourth floor. Convalescents were tucked away behind the smallpox wards. If they wanted to go for a walk outside, as their doctors encouraged them to do, they could head for the Pont St. Charles, the little stone bridge over the river, one piece of ground not built upon. First, they passed between the beds of the smallpox wards, then down three flights of stairs, and so out to the bridge, which – because it was the only piece of unencumbered ground – was hung with drying sheets. They then had three flights of stairs to walk up and the gauntlet of the smallpox ward to run, to return to their beds.

There was a rule that convalescents must stay one week after they got well, to establish their cure. Usually in that week they helped in the wards. If they were strong enough to survive hospital conditions, they were strong enough for that.

Service rooms all round the ground floor wards of the St. Charles building reached halfway up their outer side walls. Above the roofs of the service rooms the tall ward windows began. And the roofs of the service rooms were hung with drying sheets, the patients' light and air were filtered through them. A 17th century print traces those wet sheets to their source, it shows us the nursing sisters hard at the hardest work they did: washing sheets. Novices were started at the laundry of the Hôtel-Dieu, but these "little laundresses" only dealt with the smaller pieces. They worked at the river three times a day, from 4 a.m. to 9 a.m., from noon to 2 p.m., from 4 p.m. to 7 p.m. Then, once a month, 500 sheets were washed by all personnel in the

190   Religious procession, Hôtel-Dieu of Paris

La Chapelle du Rozaire

Procession des Religieuses de l'hôtel Dieu de Paris qui ce faite tous les premiers Dimanche des mois a 3. heures apres midy.
Chez Guérard.

house. The sisters standing at the table are pounding out dirt with a sort of spade. When considered clean the sheet was thrown on a table to the rear, and two persons wrung it as dry as possible. One of these, on the higher, dryer ground, was male – and he had no long wool skirts to stay damp for hours (forever, in the case of the little laundresses). In winter the sisters had to break the ice. When a piece of wash escaped them, a waiting boatman retrieved it with a hook.

This was obviously a time of flood. Probably it was not always necessary to stand up to the knees in water. A print of the river, the Salle du Rosaire rising in the background, shows the laundry platform of the St. Charles building at reasonable proximity to the river, so only sisters doing the actual washing would get wet. Much more difficult were days of drought when the river dropped to where it would be hard to reach.

Once sheets get washed in such a fashion, it would be grudging to deny them room to dry – corridor-room, bridge-room, terrace-room, the whole hospital was hung with them. Two days later the novices came back to the dried linen to finish it off. They must have been made of iron – the novices more than the sheets. In principle, only after years of this novitiate were they permitted to attain their goal, the service of the sick poor.

191   Fire at the Hôtel-Dieu, Paris, 1772

Another 17th century print shows a glimpse of the interior of the Salle du Rosaire, at 3 p.m. on the first Sunday of the month, with the sisters taking a comparative rest and having fun. They are in procession through the hospital with tapers; the rich and noble of Paris have come to watch, bringing their children along for an edifying spectacle. Those in this hospital knew how to celebrate its occasions: the name day of John the Baptist, its patron saint, was a time of real feasting, when patients got their bellies full for once. However, a hospital ordinance was considered necessary to warn that "Rockets and fireworks are not to be let off within the house or in nearby areas by officers, surgeons, or students, even on the eve or the day of St. John."

Hospitalization was livelier in those days.

The medieval Hôtel-Dieu finally vanished into fire in the 18th century. In 1718 came a warning: the Petit Pont with its shops burned down, the Petit Chatelet was singed, but the hospital escaped. In 1737 two early wards, St. Denis and St. Côme, and a chapel on the Parvis, all burned down. There were other fires too, in 1742 and 1749.

The Great Fire took place at one in the morning, December 30, 1772, and the two long buildings with their peaked roofs perished: Salle St. Louis, Salle St. Jean, and the Salle du Legat – all but their beautiful medieval stone facades. In our picture a brave fire engine is stationed on the Petit Pont, with the surviving facade of the Salle Neuve behind it, and the towers of Notre Dame to which 500 patients were removed in the middle of the night.

Such were the consequences of parading with tapers, but even more of using basements to store food, wood, oil, and wax, and for making candles. One need only apply imagination to an oil vat, preserved in the basement of the Hospital Santa Maria Nuova in Florence (the vat is dated 1585), and picture a sister with a lamp coming to draw oil at the bunghole... The vat in Florence was totally uncovered.

192   Oil vat in the basement, Ospedale Santa Maria Nuova, Florence, Italy

193   Bung hole, oil vat, Ospedale Santa Maria Nuova, Florence, Italy

After the big fire of 1772, reformers went to work in earnest. As early as 1737 it had been suggested that the Hôtel-Dieu be relocated further from the center of town, on the Ile des Cygnes. Since on the Ile de la Cité by that time no more Hôtel-Dieu remained along the river, and rebuilding was inevitable, statistics were produced to prove that the number of patients destined for the Hôtel-Dieu could simply not fit into the available space. Facts were circulated about what overcrowding was like in the Hôtel-Dieu. But the religious who ran the hospital had never wanted to budge, and would not budge. By Letters Patent of 1773, Louis XV ordered the remains of the Hôtel-Dieu razed and a new one built. The religious objected that no amount of money would make the new hospital better than the old. Louis XV died, and the project was postponed.

Louis XVI was interested in hospital reform, and appointed a Commission to examine the hospitals of Paris, particularly the Hôtel-Dieu, and suggest a plan. The Commission took the precaution of securing permissions also from the Archbishop of Paris and the First President of the secular Council in authority over the Hôtel-Dieu. In other hospitals, Commission members were welcomed. They were refused admission at the Hôtel Dieu by the religious Sisters who administered it. Entrenched is too weak a word for the Sisters' position!

The Commission recommended that the Hôtel-Dieu be abolished, and four new hospitals of 1,000 patients each be built at the four corners of Paris. Louis XVI accepted the conclusions of the Commission – then yielded to the petitions of the religious that the Hôtel-Dieu be maintained and

194   The new Hôtel-Dieu, Paris

rebuilt on its former location: "We will improve, we will perfect, but we will not destroy." New five-storey buildings were put up on the same site, behind the medieval facade, which was allowed to stand as a kind of monument until 1836, when it, the St. Charles bridge, and the Salle du Rosaire were destroyed. Nothing remained to show that a medieval hospital ever stood there.

Louis XVI was firmly on the side of hospital reform, particularly in regard to the Hôtel-Dieu, and in 1781 he issued Letters Patent ordering a rearrangement of its existing buildings to accommodate 3,000 patients, and a thousand more during epidemics. Men and women were to be in separate buildings. Special wards and promenades were to be reserved for convalescents. "Evidently," comments the historian Phyllis Richmond, "he had never seen the Hôtel-Dieu."

In 1787, the king emphatically approved the report of his Commissioners, recommending four new hospitals of 1200 patients each, at the four corners of Paris. He authorized subscriptions and a lottery to raise the money for them. A quite sufficient fund was easily raised, 1,200,000

livres, but by this time the monarchy itself was in difficulties, not only financially, and the money went for other purposes.

Nevertheless, with help seemingly so near – foreseeing Reform, but not a Revolution – planners and architects poured forth a spate of designs for hospitals of 1,200 patients, separating patients by diagnosis in wards of their own, and also by sex. One can watch the pavilion form emerge from fantastic beginnings. Most traditional was an extension of the hollow-square hospital by Pierre Panseron (1773). There were to be *four* hollow squares, of wards joined at the top by a cross-shaped church and at bottom by a cross-shaped kitchen (18th century symmetry!). The circle at the center of the plan was a pump operated by horsepower and intended to ventilate the four radiating corridors of latrines.

Wards that radiated were a next logical step toward subdivision; in Antoine Petit's plan of 1774 they were joined to a central church not primarily intended for services – it had a conical dome intended to ventilate not only itself but the kitchen, apothecary, bakery and laundry that hugged its hub. And the wards! – four stories, improbably designed as

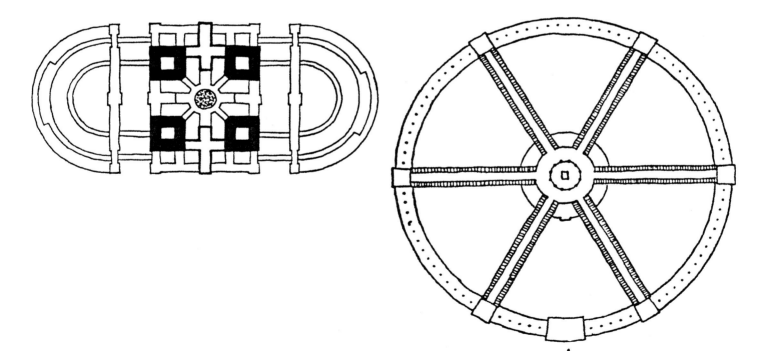

195   Project for a Hôtel-Dieu by Pierre Panseron, 1773

196   Project for a hospital by Antoine Petit, 1774

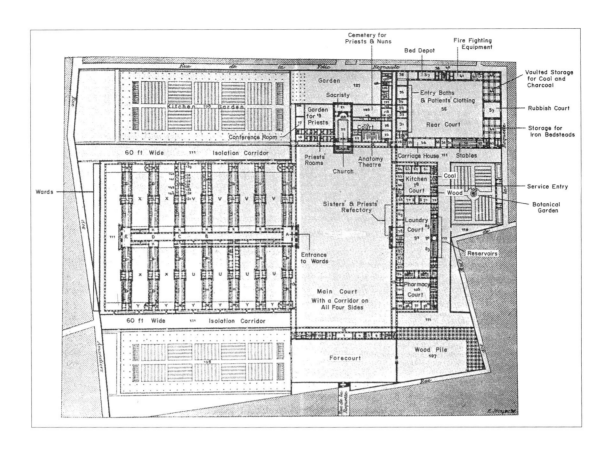

Cemetery for
Priests & Nuns

Fire Fighting
Equipment

Bed Depot

Garden

Sacristy

Vaulted Storage
for Coal and
Charcoal

Entry Baths
& Patients' Clothing

Rear Court

Rubbish Court

Garden
for Priests

Storage for
Iron Bedsteads

Conference Room

Court

Priests'
Rooms

Church

Anatomy
Theatre

Carriage House   Stables

60 ft Wide   Isolation Corridor

Kitchen
Court

Coal

Service Entry

Wood

Wards

Botanical
Garden

Sisters' & Priests'
Refectory

Laundry
Court

Reservoirs

Entrance
to Wards

Main Court
With a Corridor on
All Four Sides

Pharmacy
Court

60 ft Wide   Isolation Corridor

Wood Pile
107

Forecourt

Kitchen Garden

an open wind tunnel, with wards on the upper three stories in the form of narrow balconies over the atrium. The wind was to blow medical impurities right into the vent above the church.

Spoke and hub planning was carried to the ultimate improbability in a plan (1775) for a Colosseum on the Ile des Cygnes with 5,200 beds.

A plan of 1787 had a little bit of everything: hollow square, central court, church; *and* on half the site, the individual long wards were released from their hub and laid parallel, in two rows. Service rooms were logically placed in the middle of each ward, and all wards were connected at their ends near the court by a corridor. At the far end from the central court, each ward had its toilets. This was the first statement of the pavilion plan that would be eventually adopted.

198   Prototype plan, 1787

174

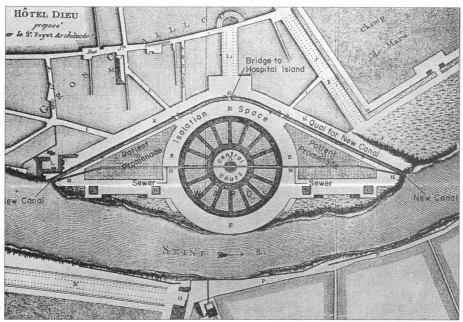

197   Plan for a Colosseum

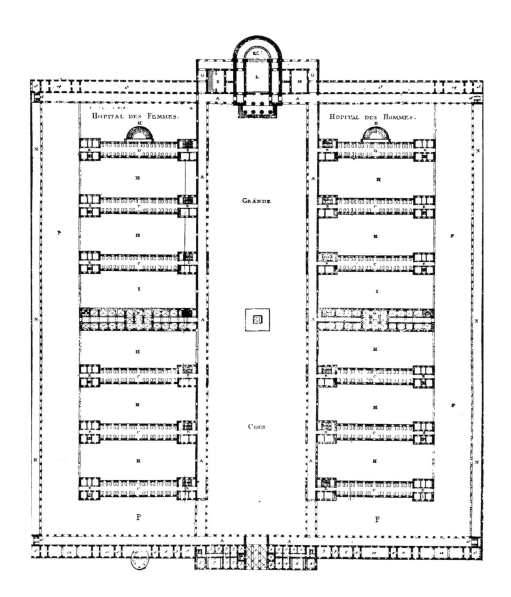

199　The classic pavilion plan, 1788

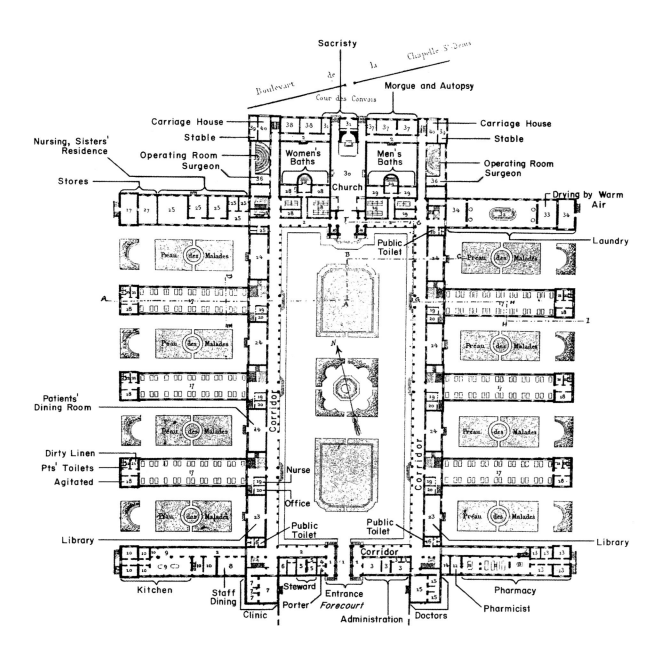

Plan labels:

Sacristy
Chapelle St Denis
Boulevart · de · la
Cour des Convois
Morgue and Autopsy
Carriage House
Stable
Nursing, Sisters' Residence
Operating Room Surgeon
Stores
Women's Baths
Church
Men's Baths
Carriage House
Stable
Operating Room Surgeon
Drying by Warm Air
Laundry
Public Toilet
Préau (des) Malades
Corridor
Corridor
Patients' Dining Room
Dirty Linen
Pts' Toilets
Agitated
Nurse
Office
Library
Public Toilet
Public Toilet
Library
Kitchen
Staff Dining
Clinic
Porter
Steward
Entrance Forecourt
Administration
Doctors
Pharmicist
Pharmacy

200   Plan of the Hôpital Lariboisière, Paris (1846-54)

But never built. In 1788, the Hospital Commission of the Academy of Sciences approved a plan for 1200 patients which had a central church opposite the entrance. Within the entrance was a large central courtyard, oriented to the sun and surrounded by a one-storey communication corridor. That corridor linked the three-storey wards, set far enough apart that their shadows did not fall upon one another. The Revolution prevented construction and this plan was not realized in Paris for another 66 years, when the Hôpital Lariboisière was built strictly according to the 18th century plan. "Too much care had gone into its devising for anything to be changed. It was rigorously respected."

201 The Hôpital Lariboisière, Paris, in 1967, looking toward the church
     from the bottom of the plan

202 Its one-storey corridor. Hôpital Lariboisière, Paris. Connecting
     corridors of pavilion hospitals involve a great deal of walking.

Finally – a good place for convalescents, on the roof of the
connecting corridor.

203   Convalescent balcony, Hôpital Lariboisière, Paris

There was a foreign prototype of sorts for the pavilion plan. Before that was finally adopted, three members of the French Commission made a study tour of contemporary European hospitals. Outside of Plymouth, England, in the town of Stonehouse, to their delight they found, already built (since 1762), very nearly the hospital of their dreams: the Royal Naval Hospital, in ten separate three-storey pavilions around a court, for 1250 patients – so close to their own magic figure! The main difference was that these pavilions were square, and divided by a wall down the middle, so each ward had windows on only one side. Sanitary stacks were not appended to the outside of each pavilion until 1906.

On our bird's-eye view the symmetrical arrangement of the gray pavilions around the court is obvious; one of them, to the left of the central church in the rear range, is now a car park, having been bombed flat in World War II. Behind the church is the mortuary chapel. The green field in the left foreground is newly filled land. It was an arm of the sea until recently, and from the beginning wounded seamen were brought in by boat to the semicircular dock, ever so much easier on them than jouncing along on land.

204 Royal Naval Hospital, Plymouth, England, 1765

12 FLORENCE NIGHTINGALE

Neither the plan of the Commissioners of the French Academy, nor the example of the Hôpital Lariboisière, was responsible for a world-wide spread of the pavilion hospital in the late 19th and early 20th centuries. Florence Nightingale accomplished that, and under her influence its wards became known as Nightingale Wards. Still in existence, still loved after more than 100 years of intensive and extensive use, the Nightingale Wards of St. Thomas' Hospital are an excellent place to view this form of hospitalization. The architect worked in response to the directives of Florence Nightingale herself, and it was at St. Thomas' that she chose to establish her school of nursing. These wards delight nurses today with their ease of supervision. But in Miss Nightingale's time their sanitary aspect was of greatest concern.

Miss Nightingale was herself a graduate of a species of Hôtel-Dieu. During the Crimean War she nursed in a converted barracks at Scutari, Turkey, and saw how hospitals by themselves could decimate a patient population. Mortality 73 percent in six months, from disease alone. At one point the hospital water supply was found to have been flowing over the body of a dead horse. Miss Nightingale loved the British soldier, as only one incapable of everyday relationships can love the chosen object, and to lose so many of her beloved, not to a death in battle but as the result of an attempt to heal, was devastating to her.

She became extra-perceptive of filth, compulsive about adequate ventilation, and years after the discoveries of Pasteur and Lister – all her life, really – she refused to believe in the existence of germs. As Lytton Strachey observes,

"If her experience had lain, not among cholera cases at Scutari but among yellow fever cases in Panama, she would have declared fresh air a fetish, and would have maintained to her dying day that the only really effective way of dealing with disease was by the destruction of mosquitoes."

She had a control population. Near the small village of Renkioi, also in Turkey and among the same soldiers, just before the end of the war a cottage hospital was erected – cheap strong huts prefabricated and shipped in sections from Britain, and assembled by British workmen. The site sloped seaward, the sea could be used for water transport and sewage disposal. The soil was properly drained and sandy. There were ample springs to the rear. Individual huts housed no more than 50 patients, in two groups of 25 with a dividing wall. There was open ventilation under the eaves along their full extent and at the rooftree, plus a rotary air pump for each hut that spouted air up under the tables down the middle of the ward. Mortality at Renkioi was three percent.

The lesson was clear: divide and conquer. The concept, in its military context, was then at least a century old. During the American Revolution, 1775, as hospitals became overcrowded, patients were piled in barns or deposited in

205   Indian Hut, Morristown, New Jersey, 1779

206   The outward aspect of irrepressible filth: one small aspect of the barracks at Scutari, Crimean War, 1854

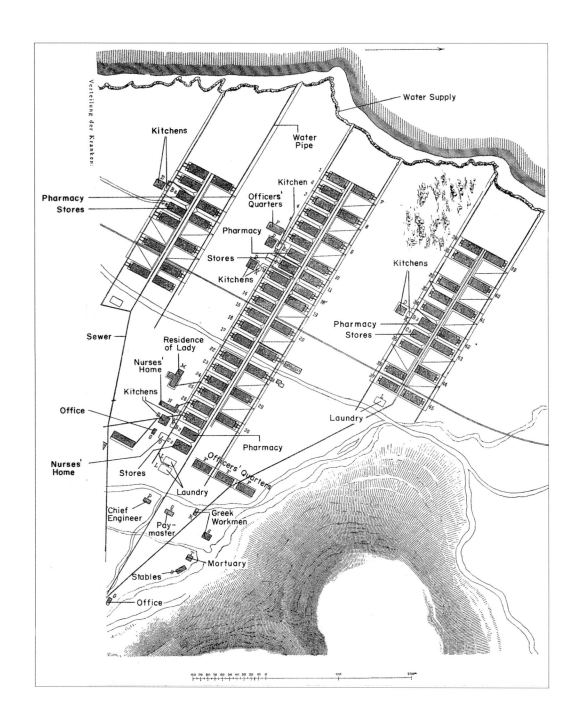

Verteilung der Kranken:

Water Supply

Kitchens

Water Pipe

Pharmacy
Stores

Kitchen

Officers'
Quarters

Pharmacy

Stores

Kitchens

Kitchens

Sewer

Pharmacy
Stores

Residence
of Lady

Nurses'
Home

Kitchens

Laundry

Office

Nurses'
Home

Pharmacy

Stores

Officers' Quarters

Laundry

Chief
Engineer

Pay-
master

Greek
Workmen

Mortuary

Stables

Office

207   Site plan of the barracks at Renkioi

184

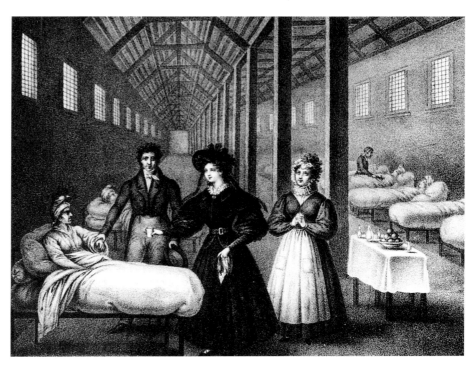

haylofts, and it was discovered that while those in the hospitals died, those in barns – exposed to cold, and inadequately tended – recovered. Thereafter Dr. Benjamin Rush advised carrying patients out to lie under the apple trees, "where they recovered with astonishing rapidity." This would not do in the dead of winter; during the hard winter of 1779-80, George Washington's army camped near Morristown, New Jersey, and an "Indian hut" was built log-cabin style, as its hospital: earthen floor, with a fire in the center of it, the smoke finding its way out through ridgepole ventilation. A physician reported, "More patients could be crowded with impunity in such wards, than in any others I have seen tried." Lest the wood become infected, the huts were intended to be self-destructible within a dozen years – to such an extent, indeed, that a reconstruction of one of them photographed in 1969 at Jockey Ridge Hollow, Morristown, had totally disappeared a dozen years later.

Here are the ingredients of Miss Nightingale's ward design:

The Hôpital Lariboisière, which she much admired, embodying the conclusions of pre-Revolutionary French planners.

The hard-won lesson of the superiority of a prefabricated, disposable small unit.

And the army barracks *per se*, a straitened long room.

Lytton Strachey also said of Florence Nightingale that she seemed "hardly to distinguish between the Deity and the Drains." Our illustration invokes the Deity more than the Drains, and there is even a hint of a Work of Mercy in it, Giving Drink to the Thirsty. Early hospital concepts were a long time dying. Note the small high windows, causing darkness to fall over all.

208 Ridgepole ventilation, Indian hut reconstructed, Morristown,
     New Jersey, 1969

209 Rear view, Indian hut reconstructed, Morristown, New Jersey, 1969

210 An actual army barracks for cholera patients

Florence Nightingale's conclusions were published just in time to exert the greatest influence on the American government when barracks were designed for Union hospitals, during the American Civil War. A little railroad was intended between units at Renkioi, but was never built because that war ended too soon, (to the regret of the engineers, we suspect). Tracks were installed for hand-carts at Lincoln Hospital, Washington, D.C. A cart can be seen under the shed of the connecting corridor at its right-hand extremity. The tents in front were for infectious cases.

211 Lincoln Hospital, Washington D.C. – a Civil War army hospital

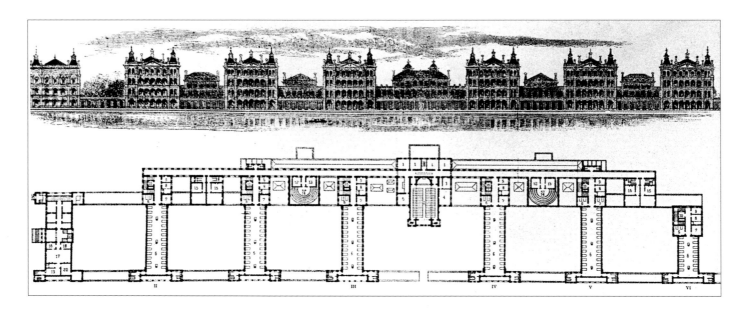

St. Thomas' Hospital, London, 1872, is a good example of a pavilion hospital, although the long skinny site along the Thames precluded a courtyard plan. Seven pavilions side by side cover over a quarter of a mile, if one includes outbuildings and the medical school. All structures were given an Italianate skin; Victorian England like Renaissance Italy required an architecture (in Ruskin's words) "raised by a mercantile community, for civil uses, and domestic magnificence." In recent times an American visitor, taking tea on the terrace of the Houses of Parliament across the river from St. Thomas', was moved to inquire, "Are these the houses of your aristocracy?"

The dimensions, however, of the new St. Thomas' were set by the pavilion system, which was based on cubic feet of air allotted to each patient, so that in sober truth St. Thomas' may be said to be a hospital built of air. The width of a single pavilion was 28 feet, because Miss Nightingale believed that more than 30 feet between opposite windows would impair cross-ventilation. The length of a ward, 120 feet, was determined by the width of the number of beds, 28, plus the space between beds, times the height of the ceilings, set at 15 or 16 feet to give each patient *at least* 1900 cubic feet of air ("in Paris 1700, and in London 2000 and even 2500 cubic feet are now thought advisable" – F. Nightingale, 1863).

The ground floor of each pavilion was used for services and three wards were added one on top of the other, with an attic for servants on top. Buildings of this height must be 125 feet distant from one another if their shadows are not to fall on the next building. The court of the central church was made 200 feet wide. It does add up to a quarter of a mile.

Arrangements at a ward of St. Thomas', when compared with those at the Hôtel-Dieu of Paris, take on an extra dimension. Each negative feature of the Hôtel-Dieu finds here its positive counterpart. To begin with the most obvious: single beds, and few of them. Windows on both long walls. Toilets and baths outside the ward, connected to it by long corridors with windows on both sides. A porch between toilets and baths for convalescents, with the best view in London. There was a staircase at the corridor end of the pavilion, outside the ward altogether.

Americans who have been brought up to believe privacy is best for all hospital occasions, who have seen only the last decrepit descendants of this ward in state institutions for the most decrepit patients, cannot possibly imagine how cheerful, sunny, and almost enticing a multiple-bed ward can be. A happy hum rises from these extraordinarily well-run wards. It must be heard to be believed.

212   St. Thomas' Hospital, London, 1866-71. 588 beds

213   Clayton Ward, St. Thomas' Hospital, London, 1971

Properly read, the roofline of St. Thomas' is a treatise on Victorian ventilation. The cupolas, styled to echo the lines of Big Ben across the river, rise as exhausts above ward toilets and bathrooms. Three chimneys along the ridge of the roof are connected to three fireplaces in the wards surmounted by three great pipes rising to the ceiling. A square cupola at the opposite end of the ward ventilates the stairwell. These three systems for aeration work independently of one another.

By far the most complicated was the pipe over the fireplace. As the architect, Henry Currey, pointed out, the center of the room was the only place left for an exhaust pipe, since there was scarcely enough solid wall left between windows to support the building! Originally it was intended that the three open fireplaces in the ward should only be used for heat, but the capacity of an open fire to

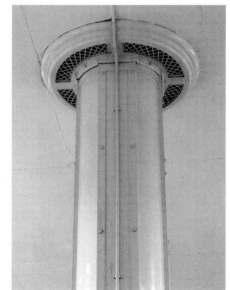

215 Roofline looking toward Houses of Parliament, St. Thomas' Hospital

214 Roof elevations, St. Thomas' Hospital

216 Ventilating pipe, St. Thomas' Hospital

draw fresh air into a room was irresistible. Some of the vitiated air, of course, went up the chimney with the smoke. An outer air tube was added round the flue, which carried off more. The lower surface of the cap on top of the outer air tube was perforated, to collect still more vitiated air from near the ceiling.

Report time goes on in the middle of the ward with which it is concerned. These patients feel very well cared for. They constantly see the nurses, going back and forth, though it may not be to take care of them this trip.

While the nurse confers with the chaplain, she can see all patients in the ward except the two behind her, and those she can hear.

217   Report time, St. Thomas' Hospital

218   Nightingale nurse, St. Thomas' Hospital, London

The porch at the end of each ward, overlooking the Thames, is easy to get to and close to supervise. Fresh air and the lively river traffic do patients no end of good.

The real drawback to a Nightingale Ward was inadequate toilet provision. For Florence Nightingale a proper patient was lying in bed well tucked-in, a horizontal soldier at inspection time. She took her cues from the military. She never foresaw a population of largely ambulatory patients, 32 of them, using two toilet cubicles. This ward is still in use but the toilets and baths have been modernized.

219   Toilet space, 32-bed ward, St. Thomas' Hospital, 1971

220   Porch at the end of the ward, St. Thomas' Hospital, London

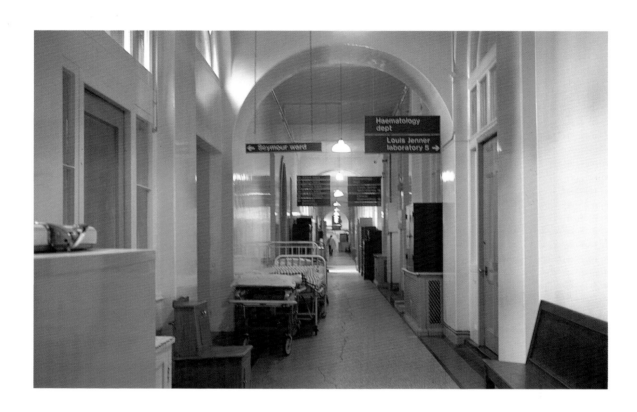

From one corridor on each floor all pavilions depended. Here medical, administrative and nursing personnel encounter one another several times a day, in casual give-and-take that must otherwise and elsewhere be planned.

Like the corridors of all late 19th century pavilion basements, St. Thomas' is a tangle of exposed pipes. They culminate in the pipes of the original furnace room.

221   The main stem, St. Thomas' Hospital first floor, 1971

222   Basement corridor, St. Thomas' Hospital, 1971

223   Furnace pipes, St. Thomas' Hospital, London, in 1971

13 PAVILIONS TO SKYSCRAPERS

The publicity attendant upon the construction of St. Thomas' Hospital, Florence Nightingale's own voluminous, indefatigable literary output, and the very spirit of an age preoccupied with sanitation combined to make the pavilion the hospital form of choice for the next fifty years. Pavilions went up all over the world. At the new Royal Infirmary of Edinburgh, vaguely Gothic in Scottish gray stone, sanitary turrets are immediately recognizable. The pink building is the nurses' home.

225 Royal Infirmary, Edinburgh, 1879

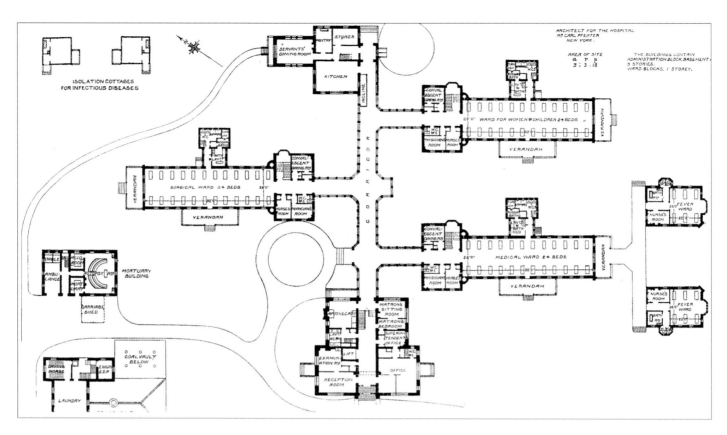

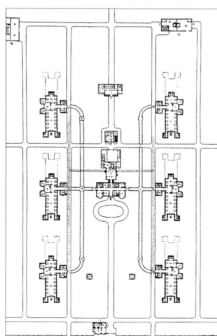

224   The plans of two among hundreds of pavilion hospitals

In whichever country it stands, whatever the year of construction, however the units are joined to the main stem, whatever the architectural style, a pavilion hospital is always recognizable by its plan. Here are three outsides (of a total of eight) and one inside of pavilion wards of the Hospital de la Santa Cruz y San Pablo, Barcelona, begun in 1905, designed by a disciple of the fantastical Spanish architect Antonio Gaudi, and completed in 1928.

227 Hospital de la Santa Cruz y San Pablo, Barcelona, Spain

226 Hospital de la Santa Cruz y San Pablo, Barcelona, Spain, 1928

228 The endless pavilion hospital corridor, Rigshospital, Copenhagen

229 How to get around a pavilion hospital corridor, Rigshospital,
      Copenhagen

231 A view of one pavilion, Rigshospital, Copenhagen

230 Bird's eye view of the pavilions, Rigshospital, Copenhagen, 1910

At the Rigshospital, for the first time, beds were turned parallel to the windows – an early approach to four-bed wards. Behind the sink, the door in the archway leads to the one single room per ward, opposite the nurses' room in the facing archway wall. It was used for intensive care. At St. Thomas', London, the single room was thought of as an "amenity room" for higher-class patients who demanded privacy, and it was outside the ward; the sickest patients were kept in the center beds nearest the nursing station.

232   Ward interior, 1911, Rigshospital, Copenhagen

233   No Smoking signs, Rigshospital, Copenhagen, Maternity Division

234   Eskimo patient from Greenland, Rigshospital. Greenland is a part of Denmark

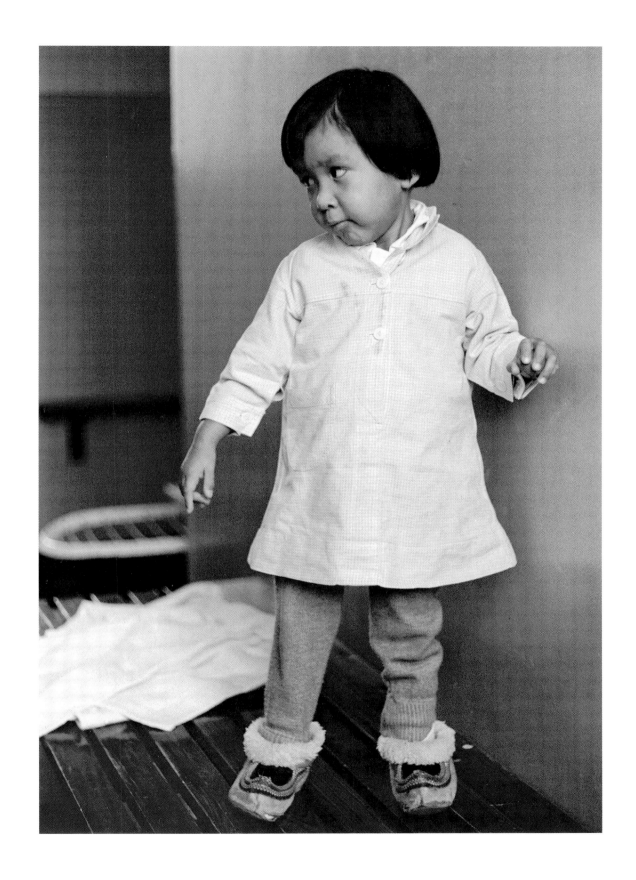

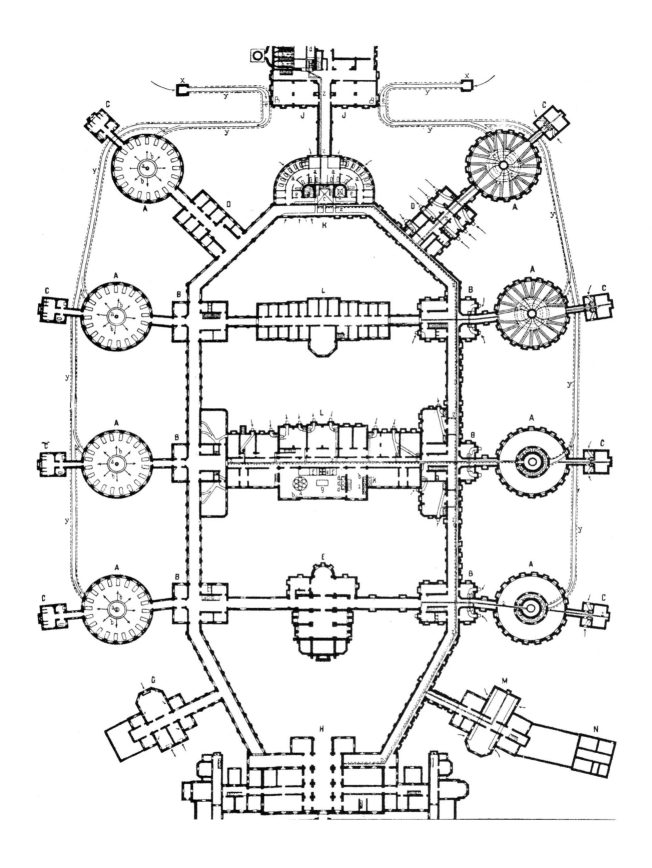

In 1878, the basic ward was blown out like a balloon, at the Stuivenberg Hospital of Antwerp. Some suppose circular wards are an invention of our own day. They say Stuivenberg Hospital may never be torn down, not because the buildings were designated an historic monument, but because they make such a distinctive pattern from the skies, pilots can be sure they're not over Brussels. The circular wards are used for intensive care, children, etc.

At the crest of each pavilion's roof is one exhaust spout, and at the middle of the wards what is obviously a center pipe and multiple air-intake like the arrangement at St. Thomas. In working wards the center pipe is now removed to make space for a central nursing station, while the ventilation holes are painted over.

236   Stuivenberg Hospital, seen from the air, Antwerp

235   Site Plan, Stuivenberg Hospital, Antwerp, Belgium, 1878

237   Ventilation pipe, Stuivenberg Hospital, Antwerp, Belgium, 1878

Johns Hopkins Hospital in Baltimore, Maryland, was shaped by the will of its wealthy founder. It was to be symmetrical. It was to be informed by a religious spirit. It was to be financed by the income from an estate worth two million dollars. It was to be quite simply the best hospital in the world.

Five experts were consulted before plans were drawn up. Their suggestions were published as a book (1875) which was of influence worldwide before a single stone had been laid. Only one of the authors dared suggest a high-rise building, on the argument that Johns Hopkins had desired a city hospital, and ground is scarce in a city. But Johns Hopkins had provided a lot of 13 acres! The others thought in terms of pavilions – oblong, square, in one section or in two. The final plan was indeed perfectly symmetrical, with a church at its head and five pavilions on either side of a central court. Oddly enough, the problem turned out to be financial. The value of the estate kept dwindling as the costs of building increased. As soon as the trustees amassed enough money to build a ward, they built that ward. But they could not fill it with patients. If the hospital were opened, running costs had to be taken from that same revenue. The most richly endowed hospital in the world stood empty for lack of operating funds. Eventually the Trustees yielded to protest and need, and opened half a hospital. When money to build the rest was finally secured, building concepts had changed, and Johns Hopkins became a high-rise hospital.

238 Façade, Johns Hopkins Hospital, Baltimore, Maryland, built 1885.
     Administration building, with dome, original male pay ward left of it
     with cupola, original kitchen (with two little hats) behind pay ward

Donors are not seers. Johns Hopkins carefully refrained from making suggestions about layout or style, but even his few conditions could not be met – he could have a symmetrical hospital, or one built from income of his investments, but not both.

What *was* built in the first great glow was elegant down to the last detail: the door-hinge in the Administrator's office, the gas lamp that has since been converted to electricity, well represent the best hospital in the world. "And it was not this or that hospital which was to be surpassed or equaled, but all other hospitals in this country or in Europe – Africa, Asia and Australasia being put out of the question." Nowadays they talk that way only in Texas.

Ventilation was a priority. In the attic of the Nurses' Home, there were, till it was recently torn down, two main exhaust conduits entering the chimney that released all noxious vapors above the roof.

But the Nurses' Home was nowhere near the challenge to planners that the Isolating Building was (destroyed much earlier). It was made up of private rooms, each of which had a fireplace with its own chimney, and there were five thousand tiny airholes in the floor under every patient bed!

239   One arm of the ceiling fixture, Administration Building, Johns Hopkins Hospital

240   Door hinge, Administrator's office, Johns Hopkins Hospital, Baltimore, Maryland

241   Central exhaust chimney, Nurses' Home, Johns Hopkins Hospital

242   Isolating building, Johns Hopkins Hospital, Baltimore, Maryland

The church at the head of the plan was one of the buildings that never got built. But a donor supplied a full-sized replica of the Christus Consolator by the Danish sculptor Bertel Thorvaldsen. The original statue in the Frue Kirk, Copenhagen appears at the end of a long nave lined with similar sized statues of the Twelve Apostles to either side. Here, alone, rising under the dome of the administration building, it casts a sacred glow in the secular space, and in its unique way informs the hospital with a religious spirit. Cleaning ladies on their way to work stopped for a prayer. A Baltimore resident reminisced: "When I was first brought to this hospital as a very little girl I was scared of the doctors, of what they would do to me. But then I thought, 'He's on my side, and he's bigger'n they are!'"

243   Christus Consolator, Administration Building, Johns Hopkins
      Hospital, Baltimore, Maryland

Today, of course, the dominant form of hospital construction is the skyscraper, where the design force is not sanitation, but economy – it takes up less land in cities; and efficiency – it requires less walking. The enclosed garden court of a pavilion hospital was a perfect site on which to build a highrise block. You complete the block and then tear down the pavilions. Here is the process at the balance point, at the Rudolfspital of Vienna, built in 1858.

A certain amount of nostalgia may be involved. The same thing happened in the central garden of the Rigshospital of Copenhagen, and one who loved those old pavilions depicted them, in 1962, as they were being demolished to make way for the block; and, fifty years later, imagined the block torn down and the beloved pavilions restored, with all flags waving.

244   A Danish dream: Pavilions torn down, pavilions rebuilt, Rigshospital, Copenhagen

245   Rudolfspital, Vienna, 1858

PART FOUR

CARE OF THE INSANE

262   Cutaway model, Narrenturm, Vienna, 1784

14 RESTRAINTS

ospice work, among the dying, has enormous appeal for people of good will, and one reason for this is that a terminal cancer patient, if pain is controlled, is recognizable as a fellow man. While consciousness persists personality is unchanged, made indeed more appealing because of the inevitable approach of the end, an end facing all of us. By the same token there is nothing whatever appealing in madness, by definition it means alienation (the French word for "lunatic" is *aliené*).

Consider a very partial summary of the actions of one schizophrenic patient (pseudonym, Sylvia Frumkin) during her eighth admission to the ward for disturbed women at Creedmoor Psychiatric Center, Queens Village, New York, as described by Susan Sheehan, *Is There Any Place on Earth For Me?* (1982): She verbally abused, struck, kicked, and

246   Belgian cage for the insane, 1889

tried to bite workers and patients; took off her T-shirt (she was wearing no bra) and made advances to male patients; floated cigarette butts in another patient's coke and drank the mixture with gusto; filthied herself and the seclusion room on her unit; talked nonsense at high speed, nonstop, for hours at a time, and threw her liquid medication, Thorazine, into a therapy aide's eyes. Several overworked and (by then) hostile employees were needed to give Ms Frumkin an injection of Thorazine to quiet her. But she did not respond to it. The drug restraint, which in recent years has taken the place of chains and straitjackets, did not work for her. Her state of health, as measured by assaultive and infantile behavior, was even worse during her tenth admission to Creedmoor a year later.

We invoke our contemporary, Sylvia Frumkin, to remind us what doctors, hospital administrators, harried relatives, lawyers, politicians and governing bodies had to put up with when they took refuge in repressive measures – many of which proved to be of equally insane brutality. The basic impulse was, of course, "Lock them up!" So the mad were locked in actual cages (Belgium, 1869), and earlier in empty towers of the city walls (Germany, 16th century); deserted leprosaria (Finland, 1687); "in dark Closets, or cold Garrets, of private Houses, uttering execrations against their relations, and the Almighty" (England, 1815). Everywhere the strong walls and barred doors of jails came in handy. In Colonial America makeshift measures gave way to a specific institution (poorhouse, or almshouse with rooms for the insane) when a town's population reached about 5,000.

247   The eye

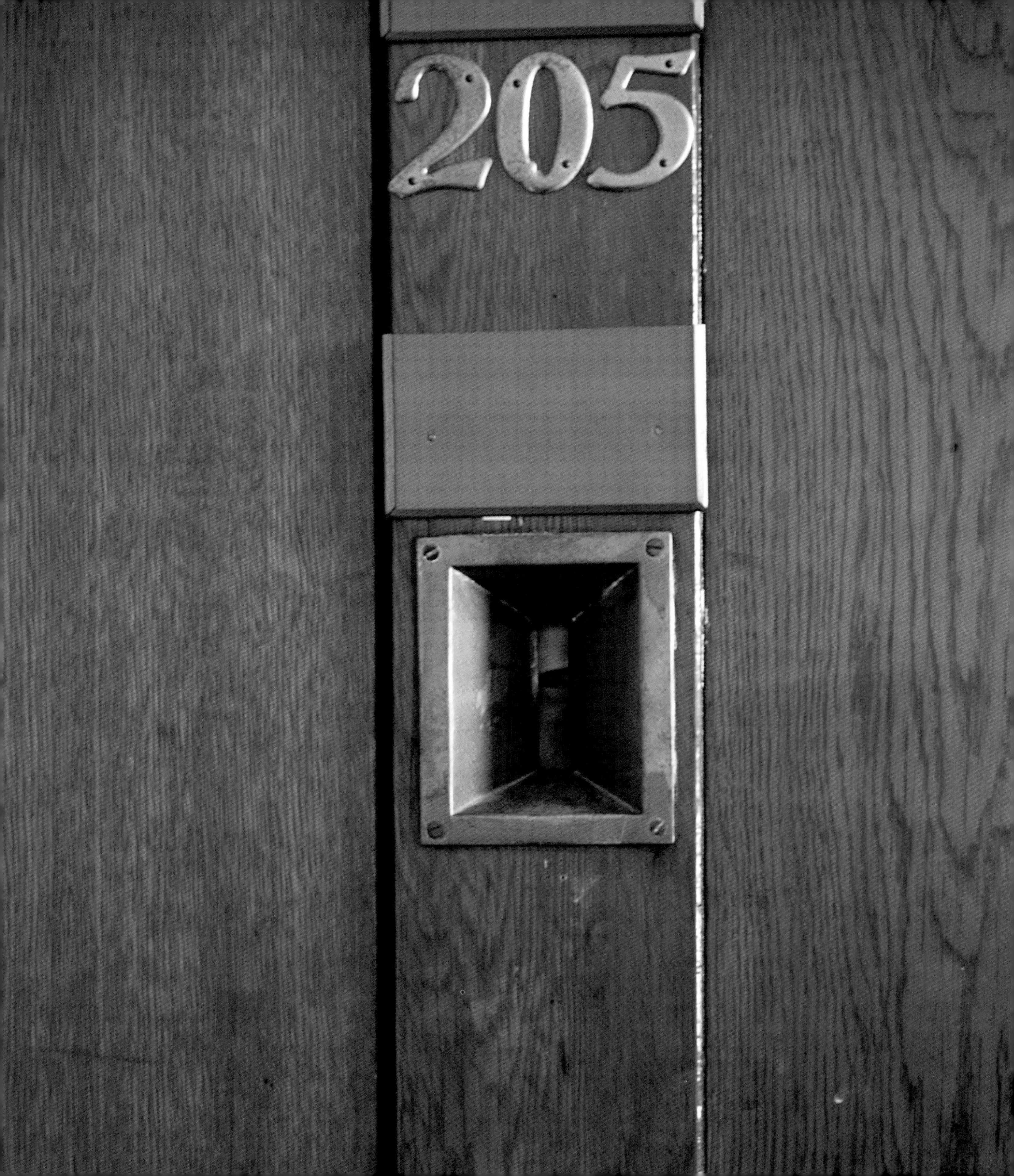
205

Cells for the insane were constructed in the basement of the original building of Pennsylvania Hospital, Philadelphia, U.S.A., 1756. Close by their outside windows ran a moat like that in modern zoos, from the far side of which the public could goggle at the occupants doing their mad, amusing, frightening things.

The insane were always divided into two categories: dangerous and harmless. Today only if a patient is considered dangerous to himself or others has he a chance of being locked up. The harmless insane (counting in all degrees of idiocy and sometimes epilepsy as well) were more widely accepted in earlier centuries. If their liberty was in any degree tolerable, it was tolerated. Today we are surpassing that level of toleration, considering what walks freely about our city streets. Madmen of every kind and degree wandered about Elizabethan England; Shakespeare made an intensive study of them. In the Middle Ages some weird efforts were made to throw the insane away altogether: they were assembled and set afloat in a Ship of Fools heading for another town, which promptly sent them back.

We have not yet cured insanity because we have not yet found its cause. In the Middle Ages the Church was sure it knew both cause and cure, deriving both from two texts:

"Then there was brought unto him one possessed with a devil, blind, and dumb; and he healed him."

Matthew 12:22

"For he said unto him, come out of the man, thou useless spirit."

Mark 5:8

In madness it was clear to the Church that the devil had entered a man and must be exorcised. Picture after picture shows the efficacy of the Cross plus a good beating to drive the devil out. This explains the treatment offered in all charity to John of God when, before his hospital-founding career began, he ran amok, "jumping about and running and shouting... followed by many people... shouting after him, 'Madman, madman!'... Naked, barefoot, unhooded, he went out into the streets of Granada, shouting, desiring to follow Jesus Christ in his nakedness... calling upon the mercy of the Lord. In a muddy area he completely immersed himself and with his mouth in the mud began to cry out his confession before all the bystanders...They threw dirt and other unclean things at him." This went on till he was emaciated and fell constantly from the blows, and certain decent people intervened.

They conducted him to the Hospital Real (Royal Hospital) de Dementes, founded and funded by Ferdinand and Isabella, the Catholic Monarchs, at the beginning of the 16th century and completed, more or less, by 1536. It was in cross form; the two rear courts remain unfinished to this day. The two front courts are exquisite.

In 1969 the Hospital de Dementes was being converted to an art museum. Its wards were deserted, though one of its last patients had been sighted lurking round them ten years earlier.

And when the hospital attendants saw how mistreated John had been, "his clothing in tatters, his body full of wounds and bruises from the blows and stones, they soon agreed to do their best to take care of him. And although in the beginning they tried to minister to him so that he would recover and not die, inasmuch as the chief cure performed there on

248   Cells for the insane, Pennsylvania Hospital, Philadelphia

249   One of the two front courts, Hospital Real de Dementes, Granada, Spain, 1536 (restored)

such people is whippings, and shutting them up in harsh prisons, and other things like that, so that with pain and punishment they might lose their ferocity and come to themselves, they bound his hands and feet; and stripped, with ropes around him, he was given a good turn with the lashes."

John protested, not on his own behalf but for the other "patients," "Would it not be better for you to take pity on them and on their tribulations, and clean them, and feed them, with greater charity and love than you are doing? For the Catholic Monarchs left for that purpose ample funding." Upon which they beat him all the harder. He vowed to found hospitals where the insane would be kindly treated.

In due time they were founded in his name.

250 Back room for patients (unrestored), Hospital Real de Dementes, Granada

251 Top of stair, back room for patients, Hospital Real de Dementes, Granada

Sovereign defenders against madness were the Christian
saints and martyrs, particularly those who died of an injury
to the head. St. Dymphna of Belgium qualifies; she is said to
have been beheaded by her father near the present town of
Geel, and where her body lay rose her shrine and church.
What healing might be wrought inside her church is
depicted on an altar screen: a large devil is being expelled
from the head of the kneeling lady; the man in the left-hand
corner, wrists still handcuffed, is just beginning to be cured,
the fetters have been struck from his ankles.

252   Altar screen. Curing the insane (16th century), Church of
      St.Dymphna, Geel, Belgium

The cure ritual at Geel followed a set pattern. Each day for nine days the pilgrims – they were never called "*fou*" (mad) at Geel – were led barefoot around and through the church three times. If the patient was too ill to come, a stand-in (as in the days of the ancient Greek asclepeia) performed the rite of the Novena. The procession followed the reliquary containing the bones of St. Dymphna. This procession took place in the 19th century.

In every transit through the church, the patient or his representative passed under the coffin of the saint on his knees – the archway under it is only four feet high.

Between tours patients were lodged at first in the church, then in two-storey "sickrooms" appended in 1480 to the tower of the church, twice destroyed, and twice replaced. In World War II their third version perished, together with the tower. Tower and sickrooms have been rebuilt, following old prints and photographs. Patients were kept in the fourth version within living memory; the present structure is fitted out as a museum.

Patients were kept on both floors of the sickhouse, the harmless insane or "*innocents*" together in three large rooms, the "*furieux*" or raging mad individually in barred single rooms, opening only toward an inside hall. On both floors there was connection with the church, on the upper floor a peephole in the church wall, on the ground floor a walk-through passage.

The accommodations proved to be not nearly enough. As the fame of the shrine spread, more patients came than could be cared for in church or sickhouse, and after the Novena there was for most a waiting period at the shrine to see if a cure was going to take place, or would last. The pastor took some patients in, but they were too many for him; his neighbors helped, as did willing householders further and further from the center of town where the shrine was – many were found willing, because these patients paid. Geel residents lost their fear of the insane, they found it very possible to coexist with certain forms of madness. Patients for extended residence in the town were picked carefully. A suitable candidate might be handed down from father to son and spend a whole life in what was, usually, a pleasanter setup than being kept behind bars.

Work was exacted of the resident mad. At worst it was slave labor, at best the patient was a kind of member of the family. To each fireplace manacles were casually attached,

253   Church of St. Dymphna, Geel, Belgium

254   Passage under the reliquary, Church of St. Dymphna, Geel, Belgium

255   Sickrooms, Church of St. Dymphna, Geel, Belgium

just in case. For a thousand years this unique system worked in Geel – some say well, because it gave the mad an alternative to incarceration and a relatively normal family life; some say badly because there was every opportunity for exploitation and proper supervision was impossible. From time to time there was a flurry of emulation in other countries; in Scotland quite a group of cottage hospitals was set up in the mid-19th century. In 1979 there were 1,300 patients living in Geel among a general population of 30,000 – at a time when faith in miraculous cures was at an all-time low. In the past the number of insane went as high as 3,000, when the town itself was much smaller.

Catercorner from church and sickhouse still stands the *gasthuis* or hospice for the sick of the town itself (church on one side, patient rooms around the court). In 1967 it was still operating as such, now the building is a museum. There hangs a painting of the ward interior dated 1639. In its upper right-hand corner, warming himself by the fire, is the vagabond we met close up earlier on. Patients lie in bunk beds, the Sisters prepare supper at a central table. There is a Christ-like figure, very tall, in a red robe, having his feet washed. So far there seems to be no reference to the psychiatric work going on in the church across the way. But the figure furthest left foreground has a red fools' miter on,

256   Ward interior. Painting of 1639, Gasthuis, Geel, Belgium

if he stood up he would be taller than the Christ. Behind the red robe is a man having something done to his head, and in the right foreground something is being done to the head of a woman.

One of the Sisters is brushing something into the man's shaved (?) scalp. Another (the same Sister seems to have posed for all but one face) pours something onto the head of a woman, something that stings, for the patient has closed her left eye against it. We have here a possibly unique depiction of a medical treatment otherwise found only in verbal descriptions. But these are copious, and many are literally hair-raising. The ancients had been known simply to remove the hair of an insane patient to give "grosse vapours" a chance to "fume out." By the sixteenth century it was thought more effective to add some substance to set up an inflammation. Here in 1639, it may have been vinegar, which is known to have been used for the purpose.

By 1705, an "incomparable Oleum Cephalicum... Best Medicine in the World, in all the kinds of Lunacy" was said by its British concocter to be "of an excellent and most pleasant Smell; and by raising small pustules upon the head, which I always anoint with it, opens the Parts which are condensed, and made almost insensible, by the black Vapours fix'd upon the Brain."

Patients at Geel can thank their stars they did not live in England in 1820, when it was recommended that a long cut on the scalp be filled with a string of dried peas, which in due time would be sure to suppurate. This kind of treatment was reluctantly relinquished as late as 1883 (!) by the physician superintendent of Bethlem Hospital on the grounds that "there was a general feeling against it, and it did not look ornamental."

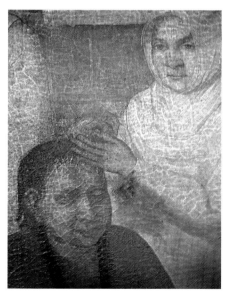

257   Head treatment, male patient, Gasthuis, Geel, Belgium

258   Head treatment, female patient, Gasthuis, Geel, Belgium

So much for the chemical-medical approach to the problem of curing insanity. Let us turn to the mechanical-medical. Cox's swing worked on a principle of extraction (1804): "Vomiting has been long esteemed among the most successful remedies in madness... The swing can be so regulated as to excite the most violent convulsions of the stomach, with the agitation and concussion on every part of the animal frame..." At about the same time a rotary machine was said to be met with in most British public asylums "that excited a new order of symptoms" by reducing the patient to unconsciousness, with or without convulsions; by 1824 the model was rendered even more effective by tying down the patient horizontally.

Now for the wet-medical. The beating that patients took from medicine surpassed anything the Church could devise. Consider the therapeutic uses of water: "the bath of surprise" where a physician walking beside a patient alongside water suddenly and unexpectedly shoved him in; "the bath of immersion" – plunging the patient into cold water, withdrawing him immediately, this repeated up to six times; "the bath of effusion" – placing the patient in a tub and pouring cold water on his head from high enough up for considerable impact; "the douche," which was mechanically controlled by diameter of pipe, capacity of tank, and size of aperture, where the action of the cold and the action of percussion reinforced one another, and a French psychiatrist said of it, "It causes cardialgia, and desires to vomit. After its action ceases, the patients are pale, and sometimes sallow..."

Perhaps we should turn back to architecture. With the Narrenturm of Vienna (1784) we are right back where we started. Joseph II's round tower at the head of the plan of the Allgemeines Krankenhaus was designed with one goal in mind: to protect the city of Vienna from its insane. Although walls were powerfully reinforced, patients were also manacled two by two to the wall in each room.

259 (Top two drawings) Dizziness to cure insanity, 19th century

260 Water to cure insanity, 19th century

Doors are heavy oak, with an inspection window. Nowadays the rooms are used for nurses. There seems little reason for the round shape other than that turrets of the city walls were round, where the insane used to be kept. Roundness does not facilitate a view down the corridor, rather it conceals one, being at the opposite pole of what is called "panoptical" architecture, in which from a central point one can theoretically see into all the rooms round the radius of a circular building, or down four or eight radiating corridors simultaneously – a plan frequently called into play not only for insane asylums but for prisons.

261   Circular corridor, Narrenturm, Vienna

262   Cutaway model, Narrenturm, Vienna, 1784

They say the Emperor Joseph II loved to look out over the city of Vienna from the attic of the Narrenturm, mounting these steps to get to it. As he heard the howls of the patients beneath him, his thoughts were probably purely self-congratulatory.

Built in 1793, only six years before the Narrenturm, the Nuncio of Toledo looks ahead, while the Narrenturm deliberately turned back toward the Middle Ages. The Nuncio, fourth-oldest mental hospital in Spain, though built in the form of a cross, incorporates to some degree Arab tolerance and forward-thinking in psychiatric matters. There is a bit of kindliness in this design.

The cross is circumscribed in a square. Actually here it is a rectangle, wider than deep, but the two courtyards to each side allowed the building to be divided as usual in the middle according to sex. At the crossing was a chapel, unusual consideration for the mad, who were generally considered not up to it. In 1969 the Nuncio was inhabited by 560 state mental patients, none of whom paid.

264 Rear elevation overlooking river, Casa del Nuncio, Toledo, Spain, 1793

263 Steps to the attic, Narrenturm, Allgemeines Krankenhaus, Vienna

The front arm of the cross, from the main entrance on the street at the top of the hill, was entirely given over to a stately stair leading from front door up to the chapel. Under the stair, in the basement, was the kitchen.

To either side of the altar was a room for patients. Men are on one side and women on the other – behind bars.

265   Entrance stairs, Casa del Nuncio, Toledo

266   Chapel, Casa del Nuncio, looking from the altar rail to the barred room where patients sat.

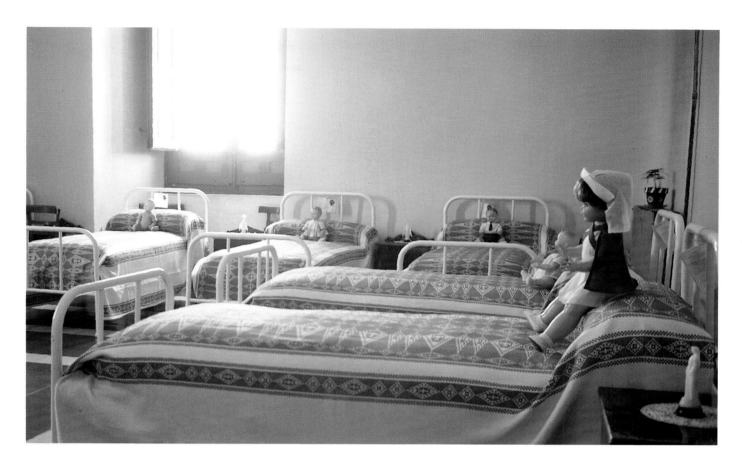

Two spacious wards in a square tower on the river side, at the juncture of the buildings that circumscribe the cross, gave plenty of space to women patients who behaved themselves; in this context, that means continent as well as obedient. Flowers were their reward, a watchful Madonna, azulejos and colored bedspreads, and each woman had her doll.

One small corridor terminating in a little shrine had single rooms leading off it to either side, with a viewing slot right over each pillow. Here too the women had dolls. Though the Nuncio was now state supported, it was hard not to see here, originally, privacy for patients who could pay for it.

268   Another tower room for well-behaved women, Casa del Nuncio, Toledo

267   Tower room for well-behaved women, Casa del Nuncio, Toledo

269   Private room, Casa del Nuncio, Toledo

Down in the basement was a very different corridor, and off it a terribly substantial door, locked at night in 1969, leading to a ward for the incontinent, in body or mind. Crowded, white bedspreads, only two dolls in sight. It smelled. At night it was lit by a single light bulb. The walls were thick as a bastion.

270 Basement corridor, Casa del Nuncio, Toledo

272 Thick outer walls, dormitory for the incontinent, Casa del Nuncio, Toledo

271 Entrance to dormitory for the incontinent, Casa del Nuncio, Toledo

273 Dormitory for the incontinent, Casa del Nuncio, Toledo

The room for baths was a treatment room, not for bathing *per se.* Bathtubs were carved from a single block of marble. Patients might be restrained in the tubs by wooden boards with a hole for the head, or be handcuffed to the shower. Footbaths too were considered quieting. This paraphernalia of the water treatment had been abandoned at the Nuncio fifteen years before these pictures were taken, when tranquilizers came in. Shortly after the pictures were taken, the Nuncio itself was abandoned. The building was vandalized, windows smashed. Still more recently it was turned into an old age home.

274   Treatment room for patient baths, Casa del Nuncio, Toledo

275   Footbaths, Nuncio, Toledo

276   Administrative nurse, Casa del Nuncio, Toledo

With the creation of the Hôpital Général in 1656 things went from bad to worse for the insane in Paris. They abruptly ceased to be homogenized in the general population or confined within small institutions, whose funds the king had confiscated to maintain his immense new hospitals. Within a few years one percent of the population – deviants, loafers, paupers, vagabonds, and the insane – had been swept up from the Paris streets and into hospitals.

Among component hospitals receiving the insane, the largest were Bicêtre for men and the Salpêtrière for women. By the 18th century there were 3,000 sick and pensioners each year in Bicêtre, and the Salpêtrière was even more crowded. In 1656 "this vast asylum for the poor, this pauper village" had 4,000 "patients" in it and by the mid-18th century 7,000, making it the largest hospital in Paris and probably all Europe. (Let us remember that "Allgemeines Krankenhaus" translates into "Hôpital Général.")

The first "loges" for the insane were built at the Salpêtrière at the end of the 17th century on marshy ground a little above the Seine, just at sewer level and subject to flooding. There was no attempt in them to separate different kinds of insanity: madwomen in chains were thrown in with the peaceable and quiet, the fairly tranquil and imbeciles slept two in a bed in unclean, stuffy quarters. Large rats came up through the sewers and bit the women's hands, feet, and faces. – At Bicêtre a *quartier* was set aside for the raving mad: 111 loges arranged along five alleys one of which was called the Street of Hell. The violent were fettered hand and foot, singly, in a cell not six feet square, which received its light and air only via one door with a single wicket scarcely big enough to pass food through. Their cots were boards that were always wet, covered with green mold, and glacially cold.

The face the Hôpital de la Salpêtrière presents to the world is regal. The church of its pride is like the skyscraper of a great city.

But in the low, far reaches of the vast pauper city, streets still flooded in the early years of the 20th century.

277 Flooded back alleys, La Salpêtrière, Paris, early 20th century

278 Façade with the dome of the church. La Salpêtrière, Paris

Let us attempt to end this chapter on a pleasing note some-how. This is the courtyard of the Hospital of John of God in Arcos de la Frontera, Spain (17th-18th century). Patients here know that they are well off, and if they lose self-control they will usually come to their senses if they are told they will be shipped to the big state regional hospital.

But the bottom line is always the same.

279   Entrance courtyard, Hospital of John of God, Arcos de la Frontera, Spain

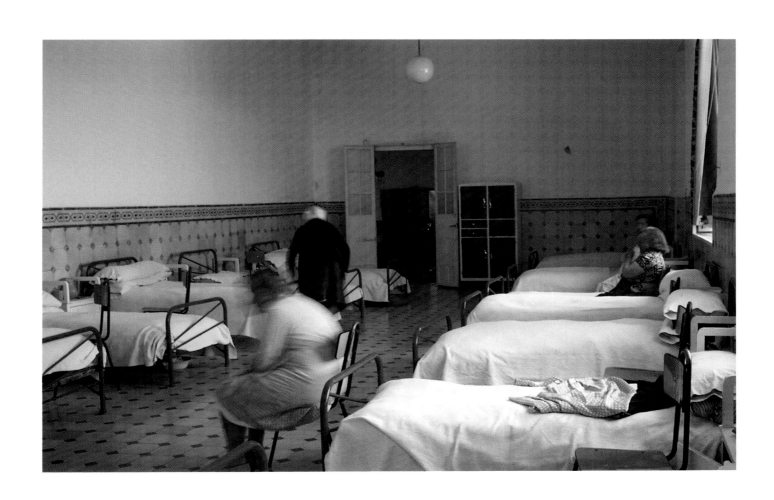

280   Inside one ward, Hospital of John of God, Arcos de la Frontera, Spain

15 THE RISE AND FALL OF MORAL TREATMENT

The history of hospitals can at least be portrayed as a suddenly rising curve, from unsanitary to sanitary, from impotence to cures of near-wizardry as medicine and surgery came into their own in the late 19th and 20th centuries; it gives one a real lift to salute an enlightened age. But the history of the housing of madness is a different story. Insane asylums started rising toward better things at the end of the 18th century, but they peaked before 1850. In that half century alone insanity was believed to be curable if you caught it in time. Nowadays we no longer believe this. The history of mental hospitalization in our time is by no means glorious, and our chronic lapses into nadir rival those of any century.

Eighteenth-century humanitarian thinking in regard to the insane surfaced in, of all places, Paris, where reformers insisted that the mad be given pure air and water, exercise, and trees to protect them from the sun. Different types of insanity were to be segregated from one another. Patients of each were to be housed in one-storey buildings of single rooms with a central dayroom. These improvements were introduced in 1789, on the eve of the French Revolution, by Louis XVI, and his court architect, Francois Viel, together with new loges at the Salpêtrère.

The melancholy were grouped around a garden, though in an 1824 painting they are shown looking everywhere but at the trees. The title of the painting is "Cour des Paisibles" – court of those who will do no harm; the dangerous insane would not be let loose to run about like this. The insane were sorted by kinds of case. An iron fence separating categories of insane can ben seen center background. The central tower was a ventilating device, to pull in air through the windows.

Ventilation also took place through the roof: a cold idea, but the insane were believed insensible to cold.

281 Cells for the insane, old style, at the Hôpital de l' Antiquaillle, Lyons, beginning of the 19th century

282 Horizontal bar for chaining the madwomen. One of the two surviving loges, La Salpêtrière

In a widely-known painting of one madwoman having her chains struck off during early reforms at the Salpêtrière, it is possible to observe how patients were chained: to a vertical bar, up and down which their chains could slide as they rose or sat.

A bar still exists at one of the two surviving late 18th century loges but, as seen in the photograph, it is horizontal; the patient chained to the bench could take a little walk.

The first "patient" at Bicêtre to have his chains struck off at the instigation of the French psychiatrist Phillipe Pinel had worn them 40 years. He was put in a straitjacket instead, and invited to walk in the court.

284   Side view, surviving loge for the insane, La Salpêtrière, Paris

283   *Cour des Paisibles*, La Salpêtrière, 1834

246

"He raised himself many times from his seat, but fell again on it, for he had been in a sitting position so long, that he had lost the use of his legs. In a quarter of an hour he... came to the door of his dark cell. His first look was at the sky, and he cried out enthusiastically, 'How beautiful!'" During the rest of the day he was constantly in motion, walking up and down the staircases, and uttering short exclamations of delight. In the evening he returned of his own accord into his cell, where a better bed than he had been accustomed to had been prepared for him."

When new wards were built for the insane at Bicêtre in 1822, they were actually heated.

In England, the first reformed Quaker asylum in England, the modest and sensible York Retreat, was also founded in response to horrendous abuses, this time in the town of York itself. In 1791, one more patient had been locked up for insanity in a place it would be a farce to call a hospital. The patient was the Quaker Hannah Mills, the place the York Lunatic Asylum, a charitable institution originally founded for patients of the middle class to protect them from the rapacity of private madhouses. The relatives of Hannah Mills, who lived at a distance, requested that local members of the Society of Friends visit her. The local members were not admitted. It was said that the patient was in no condition to be seen. In a way, that was true, for within a few weeks she died.

Stubborn, those York Quakers. They insisted on a thorough inspection. Even more stubborn was the Asylum superintendent in refusing, for he had the best of reasons: in 30 years he had turned a charity into a receptacle for paying

285   Madwomen are unchained at the Salpêtrière, Paris, 1790s

286   Painting detail: how madwomen were chained at the Salpêtrière

patients only, run for his own benefit, with one set of books for himself and one for the inspectors. Abuses at the Asylum ranked among the most horrible of the age, and we know how bad that could be. It was.

Those days, the Board of Directors of any charitable institution was made up of Governors who paid for the privilege. At the York Asylum they had to pay 20 pounds apiece. It cost 40 new Governors a total of 800 pounds to get rid of the superintendent and his steward, who, faithful to the end, made it his last official act to burn the books.

Quakers believe that in every man there is a "divine principle" and that nothing may prevent a man from obeying that principle. Insanity thus becomes merely another obstacle to be removed from the road to inward enlightenment. Like slavery, like poverty, it *must* be curable. In 1792 William Tuke – father of Henry, grandfather of Samuel, all famous names in the history of psychiatry – visited St. Luke's Hospital in London, where he saw (less than half a century after its founding as a corrective to the infamous Bedlam) patients lying on straw and in chains. "He was distressed with the scene, and could not help believing that there was a more excellent way," writes his son Henry. While the situation at the York Asylum seemed hopeless, before they thought to buy it out, the Tukes decided to create their own institution. It eventually attracted 120 patients, not all Quakers; there were not enough mad Quakers to make the place pay.

To visitors the York Retreat looked like a large farmhouse on a hill. It did not seem to be even walled. How was this illusion brought about? By building the wall round the foot of the hill, so that it still towered the requisite eight feet, but was nowhere obtrusive when viewed from the house or gardens.

Another innovation at the Retreat was the window design. No bars. They used sash windows with small panes of glass and iron dividers painted to look like wood. There were three sashes to a window, not two. The third was left unglassed so that for ventilation it could replace the upper or lower sash at will. The windows of the rear view of the Retreat look in our picture like *particularly* ordinary windows, the astonished artist stressed the horizontal dividers.

Treatment in this house was based on fear, but it was the fear a large family of children might feel toward their father, the superintendent. He must wield absolute but benign authority, and the patients must learn, like children, that for good behavior they are rewarded with freedom and privileges, but if they are bad what they want will be withheld. This worked so well that no more than five percent of the patients were restrained by any means at any time, while in other asylums each patient might be chained to the bed all night.

Every effort was made to improve the quality of the lives of patients who would toe the mark. Food and drink were liberally served; as a result, patients (like well-fed normal people) felt better and slept better. Rooms were warmed, patients got plenty of exercise in the garden and were encouraged to work. Tuke said he got pretty good results with warm baths, especially with the melancholy,

287 The York Retreat, front view

288 The York Retreat, rear view

and he did away with routine therapies of his age, bleeding, purging and the like. The reaction of a delighted public to this "mild" treatment was, "What! It can be done!"

But could it be done on a large scale? The York Retreat was relatively small. John Conolly took over the administration of Hanwell Asylum (England) in 1839. It had 800 to 900 patients in 27 wards. Within three years he abolished every mechanical restraint in the house. For restraints, he substituted a liberal number of attendants, extremely well treated and paid by the standards of the time. It *could not* be done without attendants.

It even became fashionable to sponsor balls for the insane. Here is a print of patients dancing at Hanwell on Twelfth Night, which also gives some notion of the vastness of the place. The high-class sponsors look on at right. A like occasion at St. Luke's Hospital, London, on Boxing Day of 1852 was described by Charles Dickens as "A curious dance round a curious tree."

The principles Conolly acted upon were simple and reasonable. Keep asylums small – Hanwell with nearly a thousand patients was unwieldy in the extreme. Divide patients by degree rather than type of illness: aged and infirm across the front, moderately tranquil in the side wings, refractory in wings extending to the rear. Set aside separate exercise grounds for each class. Private rooms are best for at least two-thirds of the patients; only the melancholy should be in four or five bed dormitories, they are safest not left alone. Conolly, as his son-in-law observed, "not only made the hitherto obscure movement a world-known success, but he made reaction to it impossible."

It was believed that insanity is curable if you house it properly and treat it early. Limit it to the first acute episode: you will avoid chronic, life-long illness and hospitalization. The asylum was an extension of the treatment. A faith in moral treatment (based on reward and punishment, putting patients on their good behavior and watching them like a hawk) on the part of both patients and staff created the new asylum for curable patients of the first half of the 19th century – a charged, dynamic institution, more so than it had ever been before, or has ever been since.

289   Twelfth Night festivities, Hanwell Asylum

The great mental hospital of Paris, Charenton, asylum of the Marquis de Sade, was fifty years a-building (1838-85) and it was begun in the years of optimism. In its numerous graded subdivisions it expresses French thinking of the time. The basic unit was an infinitely repeatable square of three buildings around a court, the fourth side left open. On a hillside sloping down to the Seine, Charenton is made up of eight of these on an upper level and eight on the lower. Traditionally, they are divided by sex down the middle, with a central church (classical in style, reflecting the time of its building).

290   Maison National de Charenton, Paris (1838-85)

291   The chapel at top center of the plan, Charenton, Paris

On the lower level are multiple-storied buildings originally intended for the melancholy, idiots, the senile, paralytics, and epileptics. On the upper level, in one-storey structures for safety *and* in single rooms, were to be the monomaniacs and *agités*.

In modern times the arrangement has been exactly reversed.

292   One-storey rooms on the upper level, now used for the "peaceable insane", Charenton, Paris

293   Locked wards, Charenton, Paris

294 Inside the locked wards, Charenton, Paris

Convalescent men and women were tucked into the safest place, behind and to either side of the church. It was hoped they might benefit from the healing powers of the site and its miles of delicious walks down toward the river.

A gardener of the 20th century Salpêtrière may serve to remind us that as far back as 1841 it was reported of asylum courts in Antwerp that they no longer looked like prison yards; they, "like almost everything connected with lunatic asylums in general, have, within the last few years, been made to blossom as the rose."

295   Gardener, La Salpêtrière, Paris

296   Convalescents' walk, Charenton, Paris

Suddenly, in Europe and in America, the insane patient was pampered. After centuries of belief that the insane were insensible to cold, it was now thought they should not be exposed even to cold feet, "which might become fatal to them, because of their tendency to congestion of the brain." Therefore floors should be made of wood. At Friends' Hospital in Philadelphia, instead of a sunken stone wall there was a seemingly ordinary fence, the top section of which was pivoted, so that anyone climbing it from the inside would be gently dropped back upon the ground, and a bell rung to inform the attendants.

The way color was thought of is interesting. Walls were usually painted some deep color, green suggested, to the height of a man. But in the 19th century it was proposed to give the walls different colors corresponding to the various forms of alienation, a notion comparable to the identification of patients in an asylum in Venice in 1841 by means of a strip of cloth worn as an epaulette: mania was red, monomania deep blue, melancholy green, idiocy orange, "*stupidité*" light blue, and the demented went in yellow.

Suggestions for the general patient population fade before the truly impassioned thinking about the wealthier patients, who must be attracted to one's own asylum for the early cure. There is every differentiation between rich and poor. Control, for instance, could be achieved in one of two ways: through sufficient attendants, or by restraints. The rich got the attendants and the poor the restraints. At the York Retreat there were four distinct classes, paying from four to eighty shillings per week. At eighty shillings "superior patients" were given access to a lawn gently sloping southward, with a diversity of flowers. At Scottish asylums in 1807 it had already been discovered that "the board paid for superior accommodation by the rich has been sufficient,

and in some cases it has been more than sufficient, to defray the whole charge of the general maintenance and management." For the upper classes amenities were in order: oriental rugs, oil paintings, aeolian harps in the corridors (in Germany), and stuffed birds in the dayroom – a peacock recommended as "one of the best and most easily procurable, and it looks well when mounted on a perch."

At Mrs. Bradbury's establishment near London, wealthy "ladies nervously affected" took genteel exercise amid the euphemisms.

But the upper classes could only tolerate genteel exercise. Real work with the hands was very sensitive to class distinctions. Though the majority of patients in an asylum in Saragossa, Spain, in the early 19th century, benefitted from both agricultural and horticultural work, Spanish grandees absolutely refused to touch either as unbefitting to their pride of birth. At first, even for patients of the lower class, work was regarded with suspicion by asylum administrators, because the patients would have to use edged tools; as late as 1820, it was seriously proposed at the Wakefield Lunatic Asylum that no patient should work on the grounds without being chained to a keeper; or, alternatively, patients should be allotted one corner of the garden and made to dig it up over and over the whole year round. Only gradually did management recognize what a gold mine they had in the patients' unused energy. Thereafter, for a century, in many poorer institutions the cooking, cleaning, sewing, farming, carpentering etc. for the whole asylum was largely done by the patients themselves.

Thomas Kirkbride, physician and superintendent of the Pennsylvania Hospital for the Insane, was interested in attracting to his institution in Philadelphia as many recent, thus presumably curable, cases as possible from the middle

297   The Kirkbride linear plan, Tuscaloosa, Alabama, 1860

classes, who paid, and must be catered to and reassured. For them he designed a system for a whole family of hospitals – 32 state hospitals built between 1841 and 1887 – which his own lot in Philadelphia was not wide enough to contain. The "linear plan", as it was called, can be seen at its most typical in the plan for the State Asylum for the Insane in Tuscaloosa, Alabama. It is made up of set-back segments, so that through each, by side doors at the ends of the corridors, a free wind can sweep and ventilate.

298 "Mrs. Bradbury's Establishment for the Reception of Ladies
      Nervously Affected", London, 1830's (dating by dress)

299 Pennsylvania Hospital for the Insane, 1840, now the Institute of Pennsylvania Hospital

300 Transportation tracks in the basement, Institute, Pennsylvania Hospital

If funds are insufficient, said Kirkbride, start with the first necessity: the cells for the violent at the far end. Then work toward the center (for administration) as money becomes available. At the Pennsylvania Hospital for the Insane (now known as the Institute of Pennsylvania Hospital) the ends were folded forward to fit on the lot and in an old print one can identify the barred courts for maniacs right behind where the couple is standing, with a matching structure for the opposite sex in the far background.

Circulation at the Pennsylvania Hospital for the Insane took place underground, from one end of the vast site to the other. Using a rail track for handcarts such as we saw along the covered walk from pavilion to pavilion of a Civil War Hospital, purveyors of food, linen, and medical supplies made their way from one dumbwaiter to the next – these "linear plan" hospitals involved real distances.

If you look closely at that old print of the Institute you will see another railroad in the front yard, circular, this time for fun. It was copied from a tremendously popular one at Friends' Hospital, Philadelphia, seen here in operation in 1837. How similar this façade is to its prototype, the York Retreat, built four years earlier than Friends'! Quieter patients were on the ground floor, violent on the second,

and the noisy were kept in special rooms on the fourth floor of the central administration building.

Recently a section of the ceiling of a dayroom at Friends' was removed for repair, revealing an octagonal balustrade on the upper story completely encircling that room. An irresistible inference surfaces: doctors stood aloof up there, observing the antics of their patients below, in the good old 19th century way. True, we have one-way mirrors now, but a psychiatrist is much more likely to meet his patient on the level, face to face.

In the 1930's a superintendent at Friends' got the idea to plant on the grounds the pots of azaleas relatives sent to patients. Philadelphia has a good climate and soil for azaleas and half a century later the results are spectacular. On "Garden Days" in the spring a carnival is held where patients mingle with the public undetected.

301   Friends' Hospital, Philadelphia, in 1837

302   The viewing platform, day room, Friends' Hospital, Philadelphia

303   (overleaf) Azaleas, Friends' Hospital, Philadelphia

Gardens, miniature railways, peacocks – mid-19th century planners had only the best intentions, the most optimistic plans.

But.

Insanity was not curable.

This truth sabotaged the new improved mental hospital. (Note the evolution of terms: asylum, which originally meant refuge; retreat, which meant a refuge from what the word asylum had come to mean; and now the dignified term removed from both: mental hospital.)

What could not be upheld was Thomas Kirkbride's most basic command: keep the size of a mental hospital down, 250 beds are the absolute maximum. If you exceed that, build another hospital, use one for men and one for women. So strongly did Kirkbride feel about this that he limited the size of his single rooms (and two-thirds of the patients were to be in single rooms) to 8 x 10 feet, so another bed could not possibly be added.

If only the patient population of an asylum could have been depended upon to die off, as patients in 20th century hospices for the dying do! These patients neither died nor got well. Discharges could not be counted as cures, which asylum superintendents were inclined to do; repeated stays must be recorded as one illness. As the British psychiatrist Henry Maudsley was driven to expostulate in 1879:

There are some persons who have been begotten and conceived in an insane spirit, bred in an insane moral atmosphere, and have thought, felt, and acted in an insane way all their lives; these people will remain lunatics as long as they live, will die lunatics, and, unless they have been made new creatures meanwhile, will rise lunatic spirits at the Day of Judgment.

Discharged patients broke down, returned, became chronic. The so-called back-wards developed. Dayrooms, hallways, even bathrooms for the calming warm baths were used as sleeping quarters, and treatment became impossible. There were not enough attendants – of any sort. By the third quarter of the nineteenth century a therapeutic nihilism

304   Interior of a ward for the male insane, Philadelphia Hospital, 1912

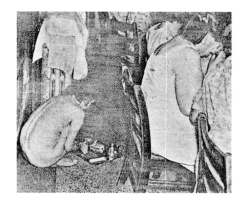

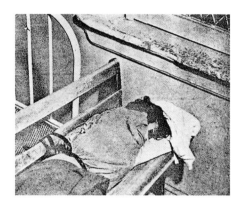

prevailed: in about 31 percent of cases recovery was spontaneous, so the average medical superintendent was tempted to say, "Oh, let them alone, they will get well by and bye."

By law, American state hospitals were forced to take in every patient sent to them. As the mandated receptacles for paupers and the criminally insane, they became mere custodial institutions in the public mind. Decent people stayed away from them in droves. Private hospitalization offered the best treatment available, but who could pay for it? Today, American insurance permits 90 days of private hospitalization at certain intervals. As the chief of her unit said sadly on one of Sylvia Frumkin's many readmissions, "The ninety-first day is always Creedmoor."

We are back on the old stomping grounds: an attendant in a Massachusetts state hospital grumbles in 1902, "They're getting pretty damned strict these days, discharging a man simply for *choking* a patient!" An attendant in Georgia

states under affidavit, "A patient who could get well here could get well just as easy if he were lost out in the Okefeenokee Swamp." The worst of what Albert Deutsch reported of American state mental hospitals in a book he called *The Shame of the States* (1948) ranks with the worst of all time.

Five years after *The Shame of the States* was published – breakthrough! Miracle drugs appeared – thorazine and its derivatives – to modify the symptoms of the big chronic illness, or illnesses, we call schizophrenia. Between 1929 and 1955, the insane population of New York State Hospital had doubled. In 1959 it began to drop. Mental hospitals emptied out and the patients were on their own, ordered to report for their medication to community health centers. Symptoms were controlled, violence was more or less mitigated. The illness however persisted. Patients did not report for their doses, and now they were on the streets, cold, hungry, vulnerable to assault or to suicide.

305   These are some of the things Albert Deutsch saw in American state
      mental hospitals, 1948

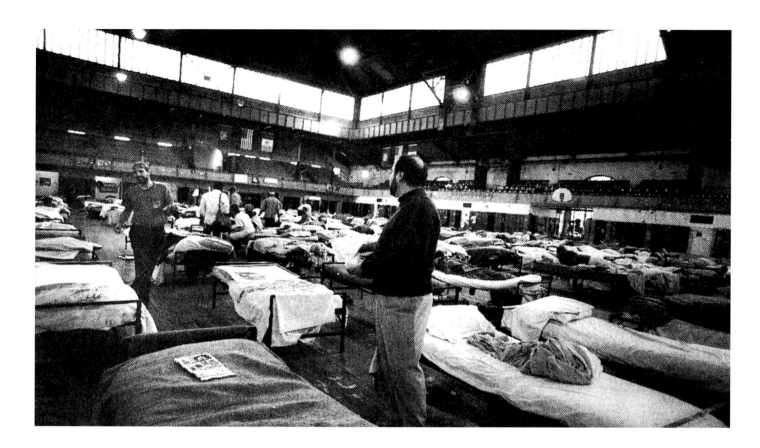

Here is a front-page story from The New York Times, January 12, 1992, with the headline: "Big Shelters Hold Terrors for the Mentally Ill":

"New York City's huge shelters for men are intimidating places for the homeless generally, but they can be truly terrifying for the mentally ill...Noises arise in the darkness, the moans of men having sex with men, the cries of the helpless being robbed, the hacking coughs of the sick, the pounding of feet running through a maze of 700 cots packed into one vast room."

A homeless man living on Haldol, an anti-psychotic drug, reported that "People get beat up here every four or six hours. Lots of fighting. Lots of violence for anything. For money. For being in the wrong bed."

"He tells himself he is safer when he lies on his side. If a man sleeps on his back... he'd be a flat target."

This is a picture of a vent man at home. In 1985, he lived over a steam vent in the sidewalk at 20th and Walnut streets in downtown Philadelphia. He was wearing a cotton jacket on a below-freezing January day. He was psychotic, and hallucinated. From time to time he crossed to the corner cafe for food, which he brought back to eat on his vent. Presumably he used the toilet at the restaurant. He could not be dislodged – the pet store tried, but since the vent man had a legal right to use the sidewalk, shortly after this picture was taken, the pet store moved. From time to time the police would scoop up the vent man, take him to a shelter and give him a bath, a haircut, and a shave; not, I suspect, without a struggle. Even in a blizzard the vent man fought for his freedom to live outdoors all winter.

But wouldn't he *rather* be sheltered from the wind and snow and cold? What were the shelters of Philadelphia like in 1985?

My mind boggles.

306   Fort Washington shelter, New York City, 1992

307   Vent man, Philadelphia, 1985. Photo by Lore Ostwald

PART FIVE

CARE OF THE DYING

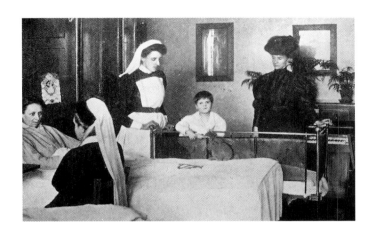

310 Women's ward, St. Luke's House, London, in 1906

16 MODERN HOSPICES

This is the new skyscraper block of the Rigshospital in Copenhagen (1963), raised in the oval garden court of the pavilion hospital of 1910, after which the pavilions were razed. How the tower dwarfs the old administration buildings, which were spared and in their day rather lorded it over the pavilions! Medical techniques of the early 20th century are similarly dwarfed by today's technologies: cobalt rays, CAT scans, open heart surgery, intensive care, the spectrum of antibiotics – all quite dazzling, seemingly armour-proof against deformity, disease, even death. Death? We can even keep a patient alive without a working brain almost indefinitely. Such a patient is about as far removed from the dying patients of the medieval hospitals as imagination can conceive.

The more cures we find, the worse death looks. Unlike those who lived in previous centuries, we are neither used to it nor reconciled. Somehow we fail to consider it as the natural, inevitable end, and blame a failure in the medical system; even the doctors feel embarrassed. Dying patients in hospitals may be hidden away at the ends of corridors; doctors and nurses alike have to brace themselves to enter that door. Cure people have forgotten what to say to patients or their families. Where nurses are assigned to hopeless cases in sufficient numbers there is a temptation to call them back from the "dead end" for cases where their actions may make the difference between life and death.

Not very long ago, even in institutions for dying patients, everyone ducked the issue. Dr. Sylvia Lack tells of a large British industrial city's terminal care facility whose reputation was such that townspeople would cross the road and walk on the other side when they came to it, as though it were a leper colony. Yet within the walls total denial reigned. "Quick, nurse, take Mrs. A to the Oxygen Room,

she's not very well." Afterwards the rest of the patients in that ward are told, "She's doing fine." They don't notice she's not still in the facility because they don't visit one another's wards. Also there is a general move at least once a week, whenever cleaning day comes. All beds are moved out, and deliberate mistakes are made in putting them back again. "Oh silly me, I've put Mrs. B in the wrong corner. Ah well, I'll just move your locker over to you, Mrs. B., and we'll leave you there."

The "Oxygen Room" being farthest from the outside door, bodies have to be wheeled down a long corridor past every ward. Corridor curtains are drawn. "But they never know. We say it's because the men/women are going to the toilet – we have everything organized here, down to the last detail."

In the 18th century they put a dying patient smack in the center of the picture, and today, with the creation of modern hospices for the dying – which we date from the opening of St. Christopher's Hospice, London, in 1967 – dying patients have returned, if not to center foreground, at least to the stage proper. Now "hospice" is a household word, and everyone mentally adds "for the dying" to a noun that in the Middle Ages meant something quite different. The international spread of the modern hospice has occurred in less than thirty years.

Respectable hospitals seem to feel obliged to list a "hospice team," called that in the United States, but in Great Britain known as a "support" or "palliative care" team, very rarely as a hospice team. In France and French-speaking Canada this service is called "*soins palliatifs*" because the French word *hospice* means today just about what it used to mean in the Middle Ages; a "*hospice*" for the dying was

308   The new Rigshospital, Copenhagen, Denmark, 1963

Thus when St. Joseph's Hospice for the Dying was founded in London in 1905, it had a model and one known by a generic name. In 1900 a Jesuit priest had begged the Irish Sisters to come tend the sick and poor of London's East End. Five of them responded, who "went down daily into the cellar-like compartments of the destitute... There was no mistaking the heartfelt relief and gratitude of the bedridden... as they felt their face and limbs being sponged, their hair cleansed of lice, fragrant night attire put on them, their pallet given an aspect of tidy wholesomeness, with the odd flower to add its quota of happiness."

A row of villas on London's East Side was donated for the foundation and enlarged periodically, till it became a warren of passages, "three or four steps to climb in any direction and ten or twelve extra doors." The nuns took no days off, they were given a two-week holiday once a year and an 8-day retreat to Ireland one year in three. As early as 1833, the founder of the Order had sent nurses to Paris to be trained in nursing of the terminally ill at the Hôpital de la Pitié – it was recognized even then that this was nursing of a special kind, requiring particular talents. Not home care but a hospital was needed, to ensure an antiseptic environment and ready source of medications. Patients at St. Joseph's, as one of the older nurses put it recently, "were like little mice in hand-knitted blankets who just radiated the love of the Sisters."

opened in Lyons in 1842 by Mme. Jeanne Garnier, but this was merely one specific use of the general term. Our Lady's Hospice at Harold's Cross, near Dublin, which was opened in 1879 by the Irish Sisters of Charity, probably represents the first use of the word "hospice" in its modern sense in English. "It is not a hospital, for no one comes here expecting to be cured," they said. "Nor is it a home for incurables, as the patients do not look forward to spending years in the place. It is simply a 'hospice' where those are received who have very soon to die, and who know not where to lay their weary heads." This was contrasted with contemporary hospitals, "cold, naked, clean, half workhouse and half jail" (W.H. Henley). Support for Our Lady's Hospice came in from bequests, and even in tiny sums from the poor, "who might yet hope to lie in the Nuns' Chapel before the earth receives them."

St. Joseph's Hospice was a major component of the latter-day St. Christopher's. Another was St. Luke's Home for the Dying Poor, founded in 1893 by Dr. Howard Barrett, who had had that sort of service in his mind for 27 years. He had begun his medical career in the cholera-, smallpox-, and famine-ridden East Side of London, but not being, as he said himself, of the spirit of St. Francis Xavier, Father Damien, or Florence Nightingale, he "betook himself to more westerly and less afflicted regions."

While doctoring the rich he had his eyes set on a class we have heard much about, the "deserving poor" ("decayed gentlefolk") on whose plight in their final days he concentrated his concern.

309   Dr. Howard Barrett in 1904

At first a doctor is in attendance at home, but this cannot be afforded for long, and he gets no better. Then he must go to the Hospital... After a long stay the hospital can keep him no longer, as his disease is incurable. But meantime the little home is sadly altered... The terrible question, "Where is the next week's rent, food, and fuel to come from?" remains insoluble. Into such surroundings a man or woman "sick even unto death" must now be brought.

Three qualifications were imposed for admission to St. Luke's: the applicant must be poor; from London; and really dying. Dr. Barrett could not handle smelly cancer cases nor delirious patients. But he would take in a child or two "whose presence softens and gladdens the lives of the others... Endeared as they have usually become to most of us, it is a sad day indeed when one goes Home. I see many a furtive tear wiped hastily from eyes not given to an easy flow."

Dr. Barrett's Annual Reports included photographs, one of the women's ward on visiting day, 1906. The seated visitor with religious headpiece is a Sister of the West London Mission, possibly Sister Lily herself, chief proselytizer. Note the cot with the dying child whose presence made the ward a brighter – and one day a sadder – place.

Patients – the *right* patients – were ecstatic. "A hospital where the only difficulty might be *not ill enough*, why, everywhere else it was, *"Too ill, we can do nothing!"*
　　"God has heard my prayer. He is giving me a little bit of heaven on earth."
　　"Sister, how long will you give me to die? I'm far too happy to die yet."
　　"I *do* hope I shall live a little longer just to *enjoy* this home."

For at St. Luke's it was understood that "even dying people

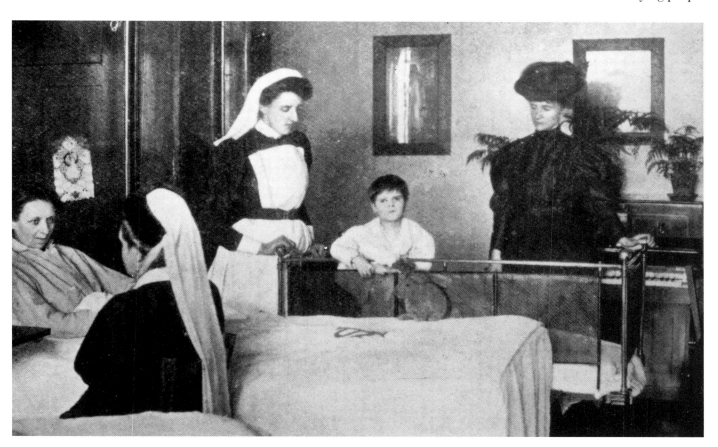

310 Women's ward, St. Luke's House, London, in 1906

cannot be always dying." The few contemporary homes for the dying were deadly places. As one lad relocated to such a place (while St. Luke's was changing its quarters) complained, "I miss the brightness. Because you are dying everybody is solemn, and talks seriously. *We never get no fun.*" Dr. Barrett heatedly denied that St. Luke's was a depressing place. "I know where are hundreds and hundreds more hidden away in the dreary streets and purlieus of London just in the same plight as those we have here... Therefore it is *delightful* to think that here, at any rate, are thirty-five (a pitiable number I admit) whom we have, in a sense, rescued..."

St. Luke's House was unabashedly religious, evangelical.

"Here is a man who has never cared about God. It is the one opportunity of his life, it would seem. Now he has time to think and occasion to think. But he cannot get further alone... An earnest talk makes all the difference to his comfort and happiness. That man can now meet his Maker and face his Savior with the assurance of pardon."

Dr. Barrett died in 1921. For over a quarter of a century he had written lively, colloquial Annual Reports about "St. Luke's House, a Home for the Dying Poor," a title intended to appeal powerfully to prospective donors, but never, never to be seen by the patients themselves. The institution was later renamed "St. Luke's Hospital for Advanced Cases," and

still later, after relocation, "St. Luke's, Bayswater" – which fooled no one, an old lady was overheard asking the whereabouts of "St. Luke's, you know, for the dying." There was always the great effort to avoid a death's-head image. In 1977 when the Bayswater hospital was modernized, they rechristened it "Hereford Lodge." And now Hereford Lodge is no more. It was in a too valuable lcation. The building has been razed and the site sold for luxury flats, to help build a new St. Mary's Hospital – its parent institution.

In the 12-bedded wards of St. Luke's Bayswater, there was a policy of regular and – it was hoped – practically undetectable movement of patients toward the door, with the sickest patients grouped round the nursing station at the entrance, so that, just before death, they could be whisked off to a single room. It was thought neither patients who were moved nor patients remaining in the ward perceived exactly what was going on.

To St. Luke's Bayswater in 1948 came a young almoner (social worker), Cicely Saunders, later the founder of St. Christopher's Hospice. She was 29 years old. She had left the nursing school founded at St. Thomas' by Florence Nightingale after three years, for a war degree from Oxford in 1944, but was prevented from making use of her nursing diploma by back pain so severe anyone else would have given up long ago. Then she became a medical almoner but the work was not sufficiently challenging. So in her spare time she went to St. Luke's ("for the dying," a great recom-

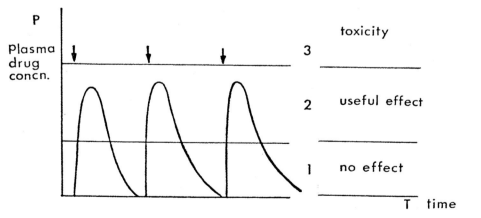

312 Diagram: pain control on demand. (D.W. Vere, 1978)

311 Cicely Saunders in 1975

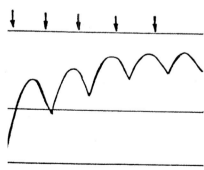

313 Diagram: regular administration of drugs for control of pain. (Vere)

mendation, the idea of her life's work was already in her mind) to take charge of the ward in the evening, take prayers, and sing for the patients in her near-professional soprano. She served there as a volunteer for seven years, when only her prompt resignation saved her from being booted out after she met a patient's question, "Am I going to get any better?" with the frank answer universally denied in this hospital for the dying.

But from St. Luke's she took with her a very significant piece of luggage: that one can administer morphine in regular four-hour doses for continuous control of pain. Doctors had been saying, as it were, "Our patients have to *earn* their morphine," in the belief that a regular dose would lead to addiction. What happens in regular drug control is illustrated in two diagrams. In the first, drugs are offered when the patient cries out in desperation. A stiff dose shoots him steeply up to a peak of relief and sometimes even beyond, to the area (marked 3) of confusion and unconsciousness. The subsequent drop is nearly as steep, through the comforting area of consciousness without pain (2) to where pain is again paramount (1). The roller coaster is repeated, the patient being usually either in pain or literally drugged.

Regular three- or four-hourly doses lift patients into the area of pain-free consciousness and keep them there without incurring unacceptable addiction. They can carry on with their primary job of making final sense of their lives, totting up their personal accounts.

Dr. Patricia Graeme, for 25 years physician at St. Luke's, was asked in 1979 how regular drug treatment was discovered there. "After all," she replied, "you give other drugs four-hourly, don't you? The hospice in those days was run by general practitioners. There was no resident doctor. Someone was always on call. So that the nursing staff was covered, they left the prescription. *We* realized how often the patient was having the painkiller. You couldn't go on giving it ad infinitum. PRN ad infinitum would have worried people. Four-hourly can go on and on.

"This, you understand, was before my time. Maybe it was happening elsewhere. Maybe it was picked up at St. Luke's because it was to St. Luke's Cicely came. No, we were certainly not actively pioneering. It didn't occur to me that we had struck on anything unusual, because it seemed to me such common sense. It's terribly humiliating for patients to ask for drugs if they're in pain. It accentuates

their dependence. But if you come round and say, 'Here, Miss D., are your tablets,' they hardly realize they're dependent on drugs at all."

To three "founding patients" Cicely Saunders gives credit for developing the idea of St. Christopher's. The first was David Tasma, a Jewish refugee from the Warsaw Ghetto whom she had tended as almoner in St. Thomas'. He was dying of cancer. She fell in love with him – as he with her – and she made him part of her legend. The whole important relationship took place after his discharge from St. Thomas', when he collapsed at his lodgings on New Years Day, 1948, and February 25, when he died, not in the hospital where she worked, but in another where she was an ordinary visitor.

At his hospital bed they put their heads together trying to figure out as if for the first time in the world, what a hospital might really do for someone in David's plight, what were his needs – and they were seen to be legion. To meet them, a hospice shadowily arose. Its symbol was the legacy David Tasma left her: 500 pounds, all the money he had in the world, with the words, "I'll be a window in your Home." What a lot can be done with a window! "He gave us a symbol of openness," she wrote in 1976, "of looking in and looking out." When, nineteen and a half years after this first gift from its "founding patient," the building of St. Christopher's Hospice was at last dedicated, Lord Thurlow turned to its patron, Princess Alexandra, and announced, "There, ma'am, is the window. The Home at last has been built around it."

After some months "of ordinary caring," as she puts it, Cicely Saunders fell in love again, again with a patient dying of cancer, this time at St. Joseph's; and again with a Pole, but not a Jew. His name was Antoni. They had three weeks. "Time... was too short to waste – and it wasn't wasted. I don't think we failed to say anything we wanted to say, nor was there anything I regretted and wanted unsaid... Our meeting was filled so full and so deeply in that short time that it gave me a new sense of time – and of timing. I know how far a relationship can travel in a few weeks; what peace and wisdom can be handed on... even in a time of great physical weakness." She adds, "Time is a matter of depth, not length, isn't it?"

You have here the germ of many reconciliations and

314   A service in the chapel, St. Christopher's Hospice, London

illuminations at the bedside at St. Christopher's – somewhat akin to medieval deathbed conversions, somewhat to the ultimate resolutions of psychotherapy. St. Christoper's staff is frustrated by the patient who comes in too late: "She died before we could get to know her!"

However Christian its original intent, and as expressed in the charter of St. Christopher's foundation, "Hospice does not try to convert!" Dame Cicely protested in 1992. "We long ago learned that God does that, often in silence. What we are concerned for is that people should think as deeply as they can in their *own* way, not ours. After all I *never* tried to convert David, and my assurance that he was all right kept me from ever worrying about anybody again – they go their own way."

Cicely Saunders was urged by a surgeon, Mr. Norman Barrett, to submerge her conviction of mission and her restlessness with social work in the study of medicine. "It's the doctors who desert the dying," he said. If she were not herself a doctor, no doctor would listen to her. So she entered St. Thomas' medical school in London, and graduated at the age of 39. During her postgraduate research at St. Joseph's Hospice, developing pain control for the terminally ill there, she discovered the love and care the Sisters gave to the dying. St. Christopher's Hospice came into being, she says, to bring together the care at St. Joseph's with pain control best seen at St. Luke's – and to keep the two talking. Academic research and teaching, plus real care – that was the model she sought to develop.

The third founding patient, Mrs. G., was responsible for St. Christopher's commitment since 1968 to its few long-term patients with the slow-wasting disease, Amyotrophic Lateral Sclerosis (ALS, as it is called in the United States, Motor Neurone Disease in Great Britain; it is also known as Lou Gehrig's Disease). The continuing presence of long term patients stabilizes workers in an institution where the chief patient population is forever being blown away like the autumn leaves. Mrs. G. actually had Devic's disease, the only case of it Dame Cicely ever met with. She was blind, paralyzed in every part of her body but her mind and spirit. "She had a delicious sense of her own crippled body. She neither pitied it nor hated it, there it was and like everything else in life could be laughed at." She was the best clearing house for gossip in the hospital. "It was so hard to remember she was blind."

315 Dame Cicely Saunders with her husband Marian Bohusz

316 "The Bird", by Marian Bohusz, St. Christopher's Hospice

As might be expected, St. Christopher's Hospice has always been a religious foundation. The chapel on the lowest level looks out on the entrance parking, and those in cars can look in on it. There is access for patients in beds. On the wall is a triptych: "Annunciation, Crucifixion, Resurrection", by Marian Bohusz, Cicely Saunders' third Pole, and first husband.

His art of high color and quality turns the hospice into something like a one-man gallery. He is Catholic, and many are religious pictures, done with deep feeling. People entering the wards at St. Christopher's look around and exclaim, "This can't be National Health!" Well, the furnishings *are* National Health, deployed with excellent taste; and the paintings transform them.

A photograph of the front façade of St. Christopher's Hospice shows the windows of the ground-floor chapel and above it three floors of multiple-bed wards – four-bed bays with colorful curtains round each bed. "It houses care and honesty in a fully authentic medical setting, recognized as such by the Royal College of Physicians," Dame Cicely proudly states. On the top floor is the Rugby Ward of all-single rooms (plus a studio for the hospice artist): 62 beds in all.

The jagged window wall is a garden space, not only for passage but for patients' chairs and even, sometimes, their beds.

317   Front façade, St. Christopher's Hospice. London

318   Inside the jagged window wall, St. Christopher's Hospice, London

Cicely Saunders calls this a "wonderful face of past pain."

319   A patient of the four-bed wards, St. Christopher's Hospice, London

Here is a patient in one of the 18 single rooms. It is considered traumatic enough for a 16-year-old to cope with dying; she need not abide the conversation of three women with cancer in her bay. *After* this picture was taken this patient went on holiday to Wales with her family, returning to the hospice to die. A hospice is a place of very late ambulation.

320   A young patient, St. Christopher's Hospice, London

Benefiting from the heritage of Mrs. G., a long-term resident
plays chess with a volunteer friend who moves the pieces
for him. St. Christopher's also publishes well-recognized
research on patients like this.

321 Long-term disabled patient, St. Christopher's Hospice, London

The Drapers' Wing of 16 bed-sitting rooms extends into the back garden. Originally an old age home for superannuated staff, family of staff, and volunteers, in residence for years – another invaluable source for staff of counsel and consolation – this wing has recently been transformed into a full nursing home. The residents are now frailer, and include as always former patients in remission, or with mistaken diagnoses.

322   Drapers' Wing patient, St. Christopher's Hospice, London

Thus in the public rooms of St. Christopher's Hospice elements meet and mingle in a constantly changing mix. Here, as it happens, a woman from the Draper's Wing accepts assistance from a volunteer, another volunteer tends a visitor's baby, a physician studies his notes, a patient with brain tumor, soon to die, holds a lively discussion with what may be a social worker.

A very important, not-to-be-overlooked care category is relatives of patients, they too are taken into the St. Christopher's family and receive needed help. This patient, let me add, was the only acute-care cancer patient I was able to meet at St. Christopher's two years in a row. Here, she had just been admitted; one year later, her hair all white, she had just been readmitted – to die. In the year between she was cared for at home by the hospice Home Care Team, planned for before the hospice opened, and put into operation as early as 1969.

324   A husband visits, St. Christopher's Hospice, London

323   One of the public rooms and its public, St. Christopher's
Hospice, London

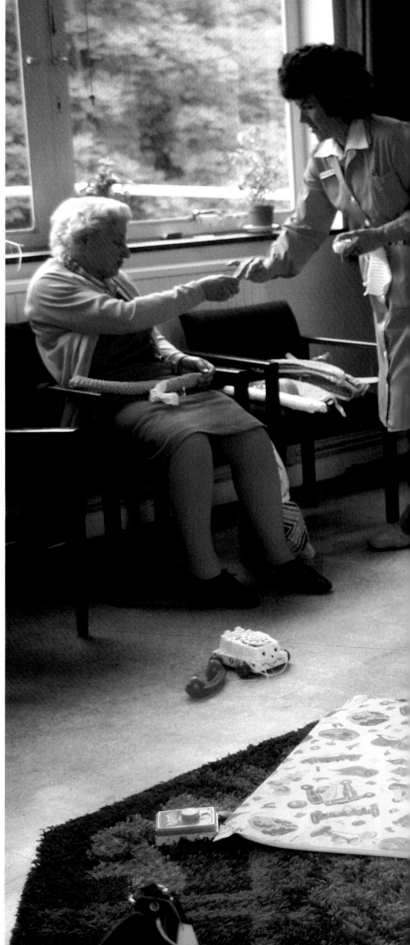

284

The youngest members of the social mix at St. Christopher's attend a nursery for children of staff. The back garden served for years as both their playground and an airing ground for patients, including those in beds. Confrontations benefited both parties.

325 Nursery, St. Christopher's Hospice

There is even a St. Christopher's poetry workshop, which brought forth the following:

PRESSING BUSINESS
As life gathers momentum
And one reaches
The Tottenham Corner of the soul
The galloping hooves are thudding
As one races for the post
Lord, so little time and so much to do
Love urges us on
You have given me peace and happiness
In which to end my days
There is so much to do
Sweeping and cleaning
To make room for You
such a sense of urgency
To commit thoughts to paper
So little time and so much to do
Lord, urge me on.

Sydney G. Reeman
23 January, 1975

Mr. Reeman wrote his poems through the 24th of February and died March 1, 1975.

326   In the back garden, St. Christopher's' Hospice

17 BRITISH HOSPICES

T he following conversation took place in a taxi in Manchester, heading out to St. Ann's Hospice in Cheadle, on the outskirts of the town. I asked if the taxi driver knew St. Ann's.

Oh yes, he knew St. Ann's. His aunt died in St. Ann's. She came in very late and they gave her wonderful care. But the person they really helped was his uncle, who was so cut up they really worried about him. The hospice staff saw him through, and he even went back there and talked to the other patients.

"If my wife died somewhere there's no way I'd want to go back there for any reason. It's surprising," he said. "Maybe it's because I lack education. If I'd been more educated maybe I'd think differently."

"I think not," I said. I asked whether, since he was familiar with the level of care in the hospice, would he go to a hospice if he knew he was dying, did he associate hospice with the dying?

He very promptly replied that he did indeed, because of his aunt, if it were not for her the word would mean nothing to him. But he himself would *not* go to a place like that, he'd not be seen dead there, so to speak.

"Why?"

"I'm a very devout coward. If I'm going to die, I don't want to know it. I'd take the hospital, and the hope I had a chance."

"Well," I reflected, "we've been brought up to believe that people who go to a hospital go to get well."

"It's not what I'm brought up to but what I've been insulated from!"

"But you know what good care the hospice gives, and if you needed it – "

"It's not nearly enough appetizing," he interrupted. "As soon as I walked into the door of a place like that I might as well jump in the river. It's quite an admission, and there's no way I'm going to make that admission. For a young person to admit you're going to die is the worst thing you can possibly do."

I asked how old he was. He was 32.

"If I was so ill I had no say in the matter, if I was a hardship to my wife and children, put me away. But not if I had anything to say in the matter. Also, I'm not religious, which

327 Centrepiece, St. Joseph's Hospice, London

328 Matron Olive Burrage with a patient, Copper Cliff Hospice, Brighton

doesn't help. I'm an agnostic, and an atheist. I'm against cremation too," he added. "They might be wheeling my coffin down to the church and I just might tap on the sides, and if I'm cremated there's no way I can tap on the sides."

Mr. Barrie J. Forrester-Smith's gut feelings are as good an introduction as any to the roughly fifty percent of British hospices that do not have a religious orientation like that of St. Christopher's (Anglican –"Christian," Dame Cicely calls it), or St. Joseph's Hospice (Catholic). "If you're religious, you can reach out and grab the trappings," as one hospice worker put it. The nuns at St. Joseph's are so much at home in their religion, they can decorate their statue of the Virgin with plaster replicas of the Seven Dwarfs simply because, as one of them explained, "We thought they look pretty."

If you're evangelical, art may ask, for you, unanswerable questions. But you can still hang onto symbols, like those of the altar-piece in the chapel of St. Barnabas' Hospice, Worthing:

"All mankind naked, with but a single goal, wherever we come from. Hands upheld to suggest that a welcome awaits us. We must all pass through the passage to a new life, repre-sented here by light. We can get you up to it, but you can't look beyond it."

(However, the present director, Alan Kingsbury, qualifies this report with later news: "...Although aesthetically it was an interesting and profound work there were a significant number of our in-patients who actually found it offensive, so much so, that they remarked on it... As there were certainly more than a dozen patients who had found it distasteful we realised it was not right for us to continue to have it on view in the Hospice.")

But what if, like my taxi driver, you are agnostic or atheistic and don't *want* to pray? At Ardenlea, in Ilkley, Yorkshire, a Marie Curie Home, there was no chapel. No prayers at the bedside. Matron explained: "We don't put enough emphasis on the religious aspect because we're all so busy looking after the patients physically. We don't you know discourage it. Ministers come in, but seldom to conduct group prayers with patients. They minister to their own if summoned."

But she said the patients were wonderful. "You get people who make you humble. They know all about what's wrong but don't talk about it, and go from day to day. They don't want to know. I feel if a patient has a pain and we

329   Altarpiece, St. Barnabas' Hospice, Worthing

relieve it, that's as much as they ask of us. It's the remarkable person who accepts, and most of us aren't remarkable,
are we?"

But where do such patients get the strength to accept?
The answer was surprising: in medical treatment. "We
don't do any active treatment here. Almost without excep-
tion they all go back to see a consultant in hospital while
they're here – they don't like to feel they've been crossed off.
Sometimes they return to the hospital for further treatment
too. If a patient wants to see his specialist we encourage it. I
think it's important to have that appointment from the
patient's point of view. It is something for the patient to
cling to, isn't it?"

330   Bereavement, St. Luke's Nursing Home, Sheffield

Dr. Patricia Graeme, retired from Hereford Lodge, London (Anglican, though she personally is a Quaker) deplored the cult, the mystique of tending the dying. "When you're dying you just have to go on living. People who are dying are just like ordinary people. People think they're in a certain frame of mind, but quite often they're not thinking beyond the next meal – day – week. All this intensity about the hospice movement bothers me a little. I didn't take up terminal care as a vocation. It isn't difficult. It really is based on a mixture of humanity and common sense. *Anyone* could take care of the dying."

Oddly enough it was the physician of St. Luke's Nursing Home in Sheffield, "St. Christopher's stepdaughter," with a physical plant and teaching program second only to that of St. Christopher's, who voiced the strongest rebuke to a wish in many hospice workers' minds: "If we could just build a free-standing hospice our troubles would be over." In 1979 Dr. Eric Wilkes stated his position very forcefully (and he has not changed his mind since):

"The difference between wants and needs must be defined. We have to think of other ways to care than an expensive private independent organization. I am not suggesting we destroy the hospices, but they are expensive, and to some extent period pieces. We've already put far too much money into expensive buildings we cannot maintain, and not enough into pairs of hands. It would be tragic if the Americans started building expensive units just about the time the British had stopped. You're not going to buy your way out of this. We've learned, because we haven't got the money. The nursing service in this country is not years ahead of America, it's decades ahead. The whole professional apparatus of care has not yet discovered that in the modern age we have tens of thousands of patients needing far more than consultation, far less than hospitalization.

I see day care expanding enormously in this country in the next decade. You put together the Thelma Bates support team and the St. Luke's Day Care Hospital, and you've got the hospice pattern of tomorrow."

Since we're already in Sheffield let's consider the Day Care alternative first. Dr. Wilkes simply adapted the idea to St. Luke's from existing Day Care Units in geriatric hospitals. Patients were brought to the hospice one or two days a week, for treatment, support, recreation, or to give caretakers at home a day off. Other hospices took up the idea at once. Actually at Sheffield the Home Care Service came later, for patients too sick to make the trip yet not sick enough to be hospitalized. At the Day Care Unit at St. Luke's, inpatients may be wheeled in to take part in occupational therapy. Patients with no bathroom at home may be given a bath. Dressings are changed, and for people living alone it means a chance for conversation over lunch.

331 Dr. Patricia Graeme

332 Dr. Eric Wilkes, St. Luke's Nursing Home, Sheffield

Dr. Thelma Bates is consultant radiotherapist and oncologist with St. Thomas' Hospital, London, and – a contradiction in terms! – is responsible both for the planning of Princess Alice Hospice in Esher near London, most beautiful of the new British hospices (1985) and for the introduction into Great Britain of the most viable alternative to a free-standing hospice: a Hospice Team that goes from bed to bed, instead of collecting dying patients in one special place. For this idea she credits St. Luke's Hospital, New York City.

What the workers who became the hospice team at St. Luke's, N.Y.C., really wanted was a free-standing hospice, or at the very least a palliative care unit. But the fact that a hospice bed costs 70 percent of an acute care bed and that is how American insurance would reimburse it, meant that any bed so designated would represent a 30 percent financial loss to the hospital. Therefore, instead of bringing terminal patients to one center, the hospice team went to the patients in whatever ward they happened to be.

(Dame Cicely Saunders has updated this report as follows: "Sadly, the team finally lost out because of finances, and only one full-time member remains. Teams are vulnerable.")

"A radiotherapist is a good person to start up hospice work," says Thelma Bates. "A radiotherapist knows about cancer and is used to working with patients. I do terminal care because there's a need. After thirty years of being an oncologist I know the beast." From the outset, she was convinced that standard care of the dying was not being well done in Great Britain, chronic pain was routinely not well controlled, even by consultants of a hospital with the reputation of St. Thomas'. Her comments and concern were greeted by senior consultants with, "Been doing this since before you were born, Duckie. Buzz off."

Says she, "It isn't easy to change the mind-set of a middle-aged doctor, who enjoys caring for his patients and is reinforced by their gratitude, and *who won't know what he doesn't know* – about pain control in particular. During my long training as a cancer specialist, I had no specific training in care of the dying, I was not taught how to control cancer pain, I was not even taught how to break bad news." Those who did *not* teach her those things are the ones she would like to reach and can't. She has given up on her contemporaries and seniors; a hospice team can catch a doctor young and train him right. There are today 160 hospitals with hospice teams in Great Britain, and 360 hospice Home Care Teams.

333 Dr. Thelma Bates at the Princess Alice Hospice, Esher, England   334 Hospice team patient, St. Luke's Hospital, New York City

With a team in a hospital we have the wide net for hospice care. There is yet another alternative: to keep the entire operation tiny, humanly manageable. Copper Cliff Nursing Home opened in Brighton the same year as St. Christopher's in London, with no connection between them. It has – or had, when visited in 1978 – 21 patients, in a converted house that had belonged to a happy family with four children. "Because it is so small," they explained, "everybody does everything, as you would in your own home. The wash, the boilers, the porters, whoever comes in does it. It's small enough so that patients can have what they like when they like." No lifts, but plenty of willing hands up the front stairs. All patients were in single rooms but the three somewhat incongruously grouped in the master bedroom, with a wholly unsuitable luxury bath at their disposal. The single rooms were so small and close together, the beds so positioned, that by leaving doors open patients could talk between the rooms. "Their little room can be their little home. They can have relatives in, and their bits and pieces. Here everybody knows everybody." Nobody felt lonesome because of a single room. "If they see the nurses scurrying round, it's all right."

Copper Cliff is not a National Health hospital but entirely voluntary. It grew out of the town of Brighton like a flower. In 1957 a meeting was called by Lord Cohen, Mayor of Brighton, to form a chapter there of the National Society for Cancer Relief. Its chairman was Dr. Jan de Winter. As first priority, Dr. de Winter pressed for a home to accommodate patients who could no longer be kept in hospital beds, could not afford nursing home fees, and had no one at home to care for them. He had found people dying of cancer in basement flats, with nowhere else to go. Copper Cliff would not take in patients who could pay. These tried hard to buy their way in, but were forced to settle for inferior care in private nursing homes. "In nursing homes, the rich don't get proper terminal care. They may get proper nursing care but there's a lot more to it than that, which they just don't understand. Private nursing homes are after the money."

Copper Cliff is still in precarious existence. Nowadays it calls itself Copper Cliff Hospice.

335 Counting the muffins for 21 patients, Copper Cliff Nursing Home,
     Brighton

336   The room and the view, Copper Cliff Nursing Home, Brighton

Dr. Eric Wilkes began his career as a country doctor for 18 villages and innumerable farms, and says all he wanted at St. Luke's Nursing Home was "to produce the kind of care I was seeing in my 12-bed country hospital, and the deprived savages in the big cities weren't getting it." Copper Cliff Hospice poses questions to both the hospital and the hospice world. With charges for service at an all-time high, can a voluntary small hospital or hospice survive? Must it subscribe to wholesaling to make ends meet?

One dispiriting answer to these questions came to my desk in January, 1992, from a nurse trained at St. Christopher's and involved in hospice work on both sides of the Atlantic. She wrote,

"I have felt increasingly out of tune with today's hospice scene, indistinguishable in so many ways from the National Health Service, and operating from a base far removed from that which inspired Cicely and the founders of the Movement... I find myself increasingly distanced from 'clinical, professional, medical' issues, and more and more called upon to restore inspiration, patients' understanding of their circumstances and needs, the yearning of carers. There seem to be sad things happening to hospice care in the States, as in the UK. In fact, my contacts with overseas hospices, particularly in the Third World, are so reminiscent of developments in the late 70s and early 80s that I feel I have more in common with them these days."

Spiritual values, that is what my friend is talking about. She has prepared a lecture on "Spiritual Care – What Do We Mean?" And whenever she gives it she is asked to repeat it again and again; the meaning may not be arrived at but she and others are trying hard.

The other thing my friend is talking about is scale. There's no such thing as personalized care on a large scale. I think of Miss Ruth Martin, Matron of St. Ann's Hospice, Cheadle, telling me in 1978, "I was asked to be the matron of both hospices, but I wouldn't want both hospices."

They built two hospices in Manchester to cover the need. The structure of St. Ann's could have been enlarged, or a double of it built across the road. Instead, they located the second hospice in Little Hulton on the opposite side of town. Into planning the second facility Miss Martin poured all she had learned from running the first one ten years. It was a wrench to give it up – her dream hospice! – but:

"You're building an empire," she said. "It defeats its object. I don't want to perpetuate the National Health Service pattern of having nursing officers in posts where they're not in contact with the people. In hospice one must supervise food, one must do some maintenance, and actual nursing care. To me the food is part of nursing, and whether the soup is hot or cold. I could have gone upstairs years ago. It would be all right if I felt I could be a leader, like so-and-so in the Department of Health in London.

"I think nurses should concentrate on doing just what they were trained for, and teach others to improve the standards.

"I would have been on the road from Little Hulton to Cheadle, attending committee meetings, most of the time, and not really knowing what was going on. I think when you get to be our age, you come to terms with what you hold is right for people. It's only greed that sets you on the wrong course."

337   Miss Ruth Martin, St. Ann's Hospice, Cheadle (near Manchester)

ADDITIONAL READING

Regarded from the viewpoint of a picture history of hospitals, most hospital histories fall into three categories. There are histories of hospitals – indeed, some very good ones – from a sociological or economic point of view. If that is the line you wish to pursue, look in the bibliographies for them. Then there are shelves beyond shelves of histories of individual hospitals, mostly drawn up for some particular anniversary of founding, likely as not by some medical man or lay administrator, wearing out the years of his retirement from a beloved institution by writing up its archives at a length only limited by the duration of his life. These authors may or may not have learned to write. If illustrated, such books are usually dominated by formal portraits of the hospital's star physicians, or graduation-type groups of medical or nursing personnel; snapshots of staff at work or at leisure; visitations by royalty or nobility (in the British Isles) which come to resemble one another over the centuries; there may even be a shot of a patient in a hospital bed. There will certainly be a full-page treatment of our expensive new machine for diagnosis or treatment. With luck you get to see the Kitchen, the Laundry, the Ambulance.

The third category is picture histories of hospitals, and they are so rare, I have widened my Additional Readings to include books of three types:

Those with interesting, unusual, or copious illustrations;

Those well-written by which the casual reader might be intrigued;

Those with bibliographies to help a would-be specialist enter the field.

I can mention only three picture books, including this one, attempting to span a large area in space and centuries in time. *Ten Centuries of European Hospital Architecture*, C.H. Boehringer Sohn, 1967, gives excellent black-and-white photographs marshalled by country, marching page upon page almost without a break. There's a sound historical introduction and useful brief information about each hospital represented.

Since *Work of Mercy* has no footnotes, the extent and complexity of its sources can only be suggested by attributions in its List of Illustrations. Materials were drawn from a dozen medical-historical libraries in Europe and the United States, and archives (where there were archives) in the hospitals themselves. A bibliography of the sources I used before 1975 may be found in John D. Thompson and Grace Goldin, *The Hospital, A Social and Architectural History*, Yale, 1975 – the third of the predominantly picture books and now out of print. My two hospital histories differ in their illustrations, not only because the earlier one appeared in black and white. For the historical sections of *The Hospital* (its first 250 pages), on principle I drew upon plans and elevations and prints as contemporary as possible with time of construction. In *Work of Mercy* I use mainly my own photographs of whatever I found on travels from 1964 to 1991, whether pristine, decayed or reconstructed.

Among histories of individual hospitals, the best I know is A. McGehee Harvey and others, *A Model of Its Kind*, Johns Hopkins University Press, 1989, which bears out its title. Volume 1 is mostly text, volume 2 mostly pictures. One really watches this hospital grow. The liveliest such history I know is *Westminster Hospital* by John Langdon Davies, a professional writer who was commissioned by the hospital (London, 1952).

THE MEDIEVAL HOSPITAL

Walter Horn and Ernest Born, *The Plan of St. Gall*, Berkeley, 1979, of all these books the most elegant in pictures and text. Three huge, expensive volumes.

Rotha Mary Clay, *The Medieval Hospitals of England*, London, 1909, since deservedly reprinted.

John Morrison Hobson, *Some Early and Later Houses of Pity*, London, 1926, for its extensive quotations from contemporary sources.

Sidney Heath, *Old English Houses of Alms*, London, 1910, lovely prints.

Charles Mercier, "Leper houses and medieval hospitals," *Glasgow Medical Journal*, January and February, 1915. Short, and brilliantly lit.

JOHN OF GOD

This material appeared in more extended form in my essay, "Juan de Dios and the hospital of christian charity," *Journal of the History of Medicine and Allied Sciences*, January, 1978. It was taken from visits to several 18th century John of God hospitals, old documents, and pictorial evidence.

The textual sources were: Juan Santos, *Chronologia Hospitalaria*, Madrid, 1715, two volumes at the Hispanic Society, N.Y.C., presumably transferred from 155th street to the Smithsonian in Washington for its Museum of Indian History. Manuel Gomez Moreno, *San Juan de Dios, primicias historicas suyas*, Madrid, 1950, was found in the Van Pelt Library, University of Pennsylvania, Philadelphia. Translations were done by Richard J. Restrepo.

OSPEDALE MAGGIORE OF MILAN

Liliana Grassi, *Lo 'Spedale di Poveri' del Filarete, storia e restauro*, University of Milan, 1972, is a beautifully put-out huge volume with wonderful pictures of the Ospedale Maggiore, early, later, and future (i.e. the restoration, headed by Grassi).

PLAGUE

Latham and Matthews, *The Diary of Samuel Pepys*, Vol VII for 1666, University of California Press, 1974, contains an eye-witness account of the plague (and subsequent fire) in London.

Daniel Defoe, *A Journal of the Plague Year*, first published 1722 and often and deservedly reprinted, is this topnotch journalist's reconstruction half a century later of the same events, more in detail and even more alive.

Manzoni's *I promessi sposi* (*The Betrothed*, 1827) incorporates in a great novel an early 17th century plague in Milan and is partly set in the Lazaretto of the Ospedale Maggiore.

ST. JOHN'S HOSPITAL, BRUGES

St. John's stunning holdings in art, many describing itself at various stages, are fittingly reproduced in Hilde Lobelle-Caluwé, *Vroeger Gasthuis nu Museum* (1991).

This material appeared in more detail in Grace Goldin, "A walk through a ward of the eighteenth century," *Journal of the History of Medicine and Allied Sciences*, April, 1967.

PRIVIES

The choice book is Lawrence Wright, *Clean and Decent, the Facinating History of the Bathroom and the Water Closet*, New York, 1960, as much fun as anything on this list. Generously illustrated with line drawings.

FRENCH AND GERMAN HOSPITALS

In the late 1930's Ciba Drugs brought out a series of small illustrated books, *Les Vieux Hôpitaux Français*, each treating one French hospital; worth looking into, especially for illustrations.

C. Tollet, *De l'Assistance Publique et des hôpitaux jusqu'au XIX siècle*, Paris, 1889, is nicely crammed with useful plates and plans.

A publication of the Assistance Publique, *Cent ans d'Assistance Publique à Paris*, 1849-1949, is almost entirely made up of illustrations, including photographs as well.

Multiple volumes in German by Dieter Jetter deal systematically and authoritatively with hospitals and insane asylums in various countries (there is even one volume on America) with the author's own floor plans, meticulously paced and spaced, maps and photographs; he also uses old prints.

HOSPITALS OF BURGUNDY

A couple of picture books with text:

The larger, produced with more colour, has written on its spine *Trois siècles d'histoire*, the centuries identified on the title page as 1667-1967; no author listed; presumed title, *Les religieuses hospitalières de filles de Notre Dame des Sept Douleurs*.

The smaller, *Patrimoine hospitalier de la Bourgogne*, no author, was sponsored by the Ministry of Culture, Burgundy, 1980. I list these in absence of a worthier presentation. Both give photographs of some hospitals of Burgundy and their art holdings.

THE HÔTEL-DIEU OF PARIS

Marcel Candille, *Etude du Livre de vie active de l'Hôtel Dieu de Paris de Jehan Henry* (Paris, n.d.); colour reproductions of capital letters entwined around contemporary glimpses into the doings of the 15th century hospital.

Phyllis Richmond, "The Hôtel-Dieu of Paris on the Eve of the Revolution," *Journal of the History of Medicine and Allied Sciences*, October 1961, a nice summary.

M. Tenon, *Memoires sue les hôpitaux de Paris*, Paris, 1788; he reminisces from his own experiences as physician there. The classic text for the 18th century Hôtel-Dieu.

FLORENCE NIGHTINGALE

For Florence Nightingale an enjoyable Life is Cecil Woodham-Smith, *Florence Nightingale*, New York, 1951.

THE NIGHTINGALE WARD

The Nightingale Ward in all its permutations, and its extensions even in India, can be followed in Henry C. Burdett, *Hospitals and Asylums of the World*, London, 1891. There are four volumes of text, in very great detail, about assorted hospitals; the fifth volume, oversize, contains among other types as many pavilion plans as you could wish to see in one place.

ST. THOMAS' HOSPITAL

For details about the architect's preoccupation with sanitary demands, and reactions in the press of the day, see Grace Goldin, "Building a hospital of air: the Victorian pavilions of St. Thomas' Hospital, London," *Bulletin of the History of Medicine*, vol. 49, (1975).

THE INSANE

H. H. Beek, *Waanzin in de Middleleeuwen* (*Madness in the Middle Ages*), Haarlem, 1969: this text ought to be translated from Dutch into English. The book contains a marvellous, original, unique collection of reproductions in black-and-white (with a few pages in colour).

Burdett, *Hospitals and Asylums of the World*, Volume 2, deals extensively with "Asylum Construction, Plans, and Bibliography" – 50 double-column pages of bibliography.

Richard Hunter and Ida Macalpine, *Three Hundred Years of Psychiatry, 1535-1860*, 1963, is the volume of choice for text, a superb collection of pointed and illuminating excerpts (1107 pages).

On Geel alone, a further treatment in Grace Goldin, "A painting in Gheel," *Journal of the History of Medicine and Allied Sciences*, October 1971.

BRITISH HOSPICES

The history of the modern British hospice is too new to have been summarized effectively. Materials on individual institutions and efforts are as numerous as the institutions themselves plus caretakers. A serious student can seek what evidence there is at the Study Centre Library, St. Christopher's Hospice, 51-59 Lawrie Park Road, London SE26 6DZ. When St. Luke's Bayswater (Hereford Lodge) was absorbed into St. Mary's Hospital, Dr. Barrett's surviving copies of the Annual Reports were, in Dame Cicely's word, "ditched." Her resume of the high points in them, and six original copies, are on file at the Study Centre.

For Dame Cicely herself, the biography so far is Shirley du Boulay, *Cicely Saunders, Founder of the Modern Hospice Movement*, Hodder and Stoughton, 1984.

LIST OF ILLUSTRATIONS

Unless otherwise stated, all photographs by Grace Goldin. Dates in italics indicate when photgraphs were taken.

Frontispiece
Archives, Ospedale degli'Innocenti, Florence, Italy (building completed 1450) *1970*

1 Refectory, Hospital of the Knights of St. John of Jerusalem, Acco (Acre), Israel, 13th century, *1970*
2 Rear wall, Hospital del Marcos, Gandía, Spain, *1968*
3 Ospedale di Sant'Antonio, Lastra-Signa, Italy, 1411, *1972*
4 River façade, Hôpital de St. Esprit, Besançon, France, 15th century, *1971*
5 Heilig-Geist Spital, Nürnberg, Germany, original buildings before total destruction in World War II, 1339. Source untraced
6 Heilig-Geist Spital, Nürnberg, Germany, rebuilt after World War II, *1966*
7 Hospital, Montblanch, Spain, 16th century, *!968*
8 Courtyard, Hospital de la Caridad, Seville, Spain (founded 1664), *1968*
9 Washerwoman, Hospital del Rey, Burgos, Spain, *1968*
10 The *Ambulance* (field hospital) of St. Claude-les-Besançon, France. National Library of Medicine, Washington DC
11 "The Fourth Work of Mercy is to Visit the Sick," by Philippe Thomassin, end of 16th century. Fry Print Collection, Yale University Medical School Library
12 John of God washes the feet of the Christ. Juan Santos, *Chronologia Hospitalaria de San Juan de Dios*, Madrid, 1715
13 Room where the feet of the poor were washed on Maunday Thursday, L'infirmerie, Byloke Hospital, Ghent, Belgium, 17th century, *1965*
14 The Seven Works of Mercy, an early English text, Sidney Heath, *Old English Houses of Alms*, p. 29, London, Francis Griffiths, 1910
15 Hospital ward, pen-and-wash drawing by Johannes van Straaten, 16th century. Wellcome Library, London
16 Vagabond at the Gasthuis, Geel, Belgium, from a painting dated 1639
17 God the Father welcoming in His poor, pharmacy, Hôpital St. Jacques, Besançon, France, 1709, *1971*
18 Founders' arms, Hospital de la Caridad, Seville, Spain, *1968*
19 Skull said to be that of St Elizabeth of Hungary, nuns' chapel, Elizabeth Spital,Vienna, *1972*
20 14th century hospital bed, chapel, Ospedale del Ceppo, Pistoia, Italy, *1970*
21 Virgin and Child on the front door handle, Potterie Hospital, Bruges, Belgium (date 1530 – courtesy H. Lobelle-Caluwé), *1965*, (printed by Sarah Van Kueren)
22 Death of a good woman, Hospital de la Santa Creu, Barcelona, Spain, 1635, *1968*
23 Death of a wicked man, Hospital de la Santa Creu, Barcelona, Spain, 1635. Photo: J. Francés, courtesy of Manuel Jorba
24 Deathbed conversion, Hospital de la Santa Creu, Barcelona, Spain. Photo: J. Francés
25 Ward interior, Hôpital Notre Dame des Fontenilles, Tonnerre, France, 1293, *1967*
26 Vaulting (left to right) of chapel and ward, Hôpital des Fontenilles, Tonnerre, France
27 Windows (left to right) of chapel and ward, Hôpital des Fontenilles, Tonnerre, France
28 Marguerite de Bourgogne, in original stained glass once over the altar, Hôpital des Fontenilles, Tonnerre, France

29 Queen Marguerite de Bourgogne supervises patients at the Hôpital des Fontenilles, drawing by Viollet-le-Duc in C. Tollet, *De l'Assistance Publique et des Hôpitaux jusqu'au XIXe siècle*, Paris, 1892, p. 58
30 Drainage holes, Hôpital des Fontenilles, Tonnerre, France
31 Rear view, peaked roof, Hôpital des Fontenilles, Tonnerre, France
32 Ventilation holes, ward ceiling, Hôpital des Fontenilles, Tonnerre, France
33 Sundial, Hôpital des Fontenilles, Tonnerre, France
34 Looking from ward to chapel, Hôtel-Dieu, Beaune, France, 1443, *1967*
35 St. Petronilla's Hospital, Bury St. Edmond's, England, 14th century. Rotha Mary Clay, *The Medieval Hospitals of England*, p. 256, London, 1909
36 St. Catherinagasthuis, as seen in the canal, Gouda, Netherlands, 1665, *1975*
37 Church of the Holy Ghost, Copenhagen, Denmark, 15th-16th century, *1965*
38 Southern façade, Salle des Morts, Abbey of Ourscamp, France, 1210, *1967*
39 Interior, Salle des Morts, Abbey of Ourscamp, France
40 Deathbed confession and burying the dead, 17th century oil paintings in St. Jacob's Church, Bruges (attributed to J. van Oost the Elder, "doubtful" – Lobelle-Caluwé)
41 Rooftops, Hospices Civils, Strasbourg, France, 18th century, *1975*
42 Chapel of the First Hospital (c. 1118) as it appeared on a plan, 1548, Hospices Civils, Strasbourg, France. *L'Hôpital de Strasbourg, les plus anciens documents*, Strasbourg, n.d.
43 The Second Hospital, 1316, Hospices Civils, Strasbourg, France. *L'Hôpital de Strasbourg, les plus anciens documents*, Strasbourg, n.d.
44 The Third Hospital, 1576, Hospices Civils, Strasbourg, France. *L'Hôpital de Strasbourg, les plus anciens documents*, Strasbourg, n.d.
45 The Third Hospital, 1673, Hospices Civils, Strasbourg, France. Agnes Goldbach-Luttenbacher, *L'Hôpital des bourgeois de Strasbourg au XVIIIme siècle*, Strasbourg, 1962
46 The Fourth Hospital in 1975
47 Interior, servant's room, Hospices Civils, Strasbourg, France, *1975*
48 Servants' corridor, Hospices Civils, Strasbourg, France
49 Grand staircase, Hospices Civils, Strasbourg, France, 18th century
50 One map of the holdings of St Pieters-en-Bloklands Gasthuis, Amersfoort, Netherlands. Book of maps in St. Pieters' possession
51 Wine cellar, Hospices Civils, Strasbourg, France, *1975*
52 John of God weeps with compassion, altar, chapel, Hospital de S. Juan de Dios, Antequera, Spain. Date of main court 1790, *1968*
53 Court, looking toward dome of church, Hospital de S. Juan de Dios, Antequera, Spain
54 John of God returning courtesy for affront, fresco, first court, old Hospital de S. Juan de Dios, Granada, Spain. Date of main court 1791, *1968*
55 Funerary urn of John of God, church, Hospital de S. Juan de Dios, Granada, Spain, *1968*
56 Hospital de S. Juan de Dios, Lucena, Spain, date of main court 1794, *1972*
57 Fountain in the centre of the court, Hospital de S. Juan de Dios, Lucena, Spain, *1972*
58 Smelly sink, ward of Hospital de S. Juan de Dios, Lucena, Spain, *1972*
59 Court, looking toward ward building, Hospital de S. Juan de Dios, Antequera, Spain, 1790, *1968*
60 Wood yard, Hospital de S. Juan de Dios, Jaen, Spain, *1972*
61 Kitchen, Hospital de S. Juan de Dios, Jaen, Spain, *1972*
62 Cross-shaped hospital plan, Hospital de Santa Cruz, Toledo, by Enrique Egas, 1504-1514, from George Kubler and Martin Soria, *Art and Architecture in Spain and Portugal...1580-1800*, Penguin, 1969.

INDEX

DATE DUE			